A BAKER'S FIELD GUIDE

Cupcakes

Deliciously Decorated Crowd Pleasers
for Parties and Holidays

DEDE WILSON

THE HARVARD COMMON PRESS

Boston, Massachusetts

THE HARVARD COMMON PRESS

535 Albany Street
Boston, Massachusetts 02118
www.harvardcommonpress.com

Printed in China
Printed on acid-free paper

The Library of Congress has cataloged the original edition as follows:

Wilson, Dede.
    A baker's field guide to cupcakes : deliciously decorated crowd
pleasers for parties and holidays / Dede Wilson.
        p. cm.
    Includes index.
    ISBN 1-55832-323-6 (hardcover : alk. paper)
1. Cake. 2. Holiday cookery. I. Title.
    TX771.W465 2006
    641.8'653—dc22

                                                                    2006002861

Reprint ISBN: 978-1-55832-752-8 (pbk.)

Special bulk-order discounts are available on this and other
Harvard Common Press books. Companies and organizations may
purchase books for premiums or resale, or may arrange a custom
edition, by contacting the Marketing Director at the address above.

Book design by Night & Day Design
Cover and interior photographs by Eric Roth Photography
Cupcake preparation and styling by Mary Bandereck

10 9 8 7 6 5 4 3 2 1

This one's for you, Ravenna. My one

and only daughter—beauty and brains

have never found a better home.

Contents

Acknowledgments

Sometimes a person comes into your life in a surprising way and brings unexpected benefits! Such was the case with Amie Richan. She patiently waited on line at a book signing to meet me—and we immediately started chatting about buttercreams and cakes, design ideas, and the baking projects we were each working on. Her brilliant ideas have left an indelible stamp on this book. I met her right when I was beginning the recipe development process for this book and picked her brain for flavor and design ideas—and boy, was she full of them! Amie, thank you from the bottom of my heart. Enthusiastic home bakers such as you are whom these books are for—cupcake hugs and kisses to you and your family.

The folks at The Harvard Common Press always keep the pages turning: Bruce Shaw, publisher; Christine Alaimo, associate publisher; Valerie Cimino, executive editor; Virginia Downes, production manager; Christine Corcoran Cox, managing editor; Pat Jalbert-Levine, project manager; Abby Collier, production editor; Liza Beth, publicity manager; Betsy Young, sales director; Amy Etcheson, marketing associate; Megan Weireter, special sales associate; Ellie Levine, office manager. Also, thanks to the two folks who make these books appeal to so many—photographer Eric Roth and food stylist Mary Bandereck.

Thank you to my literary agents, Maureen and Eric Lasher, who always provide inspired guidance.

Thank you to Jered Thorp and Wilton for helping with equipment and supplies.

Thank you to my twins, Freeman and Forrester, for testing and carrying dozens of cupcakes to school for sampling.

Thanks to Mary McNamara, my baking muse and sounding board, and to Juanita Plimpton for keeping my sanity intact and providing daily intellectual stimulation.

And to David: I love you.

Introduction

Welcome to the fourth Baker's Field Guide—this one featuring cupcakes! These individual treats are easy and fun to bake, and they suit many occasions, from birthdays to picnics, office parties to bake sales, and maybe even some that you haven't thought of before. How about a cupcake tower for a bridal shower? Or a bittersweet chocolate extravaganza for October 18, which is, believe it or not, National Chocolate Cupcake Day?

Cupcakes are, of course, small cakes, plain and simple, and therein lies their charm. Each individual cupcake is yours alone to be enjoyed—no need to share! All of that cake and frosting is just for you—and it's just enough to feel slightly indulgent without going over the top. And I bet that the act of peeling away the paper cupcake liner will immediately take you back to childhood and a simpler time when eating a cupcake was pure joy. That delight can be recaptured through these recipes—for folks of any age—and I promise that your lucky friends and family will greet your platter of cupcakes with a grin from ear to ear.

Happy baking!

How to Use This Book

This book accompanies *A Baker's Field Guide to Christmas Cookies*, *A Baker's Field Guide to Chocolate Chip Cookies*, and *A Baker's Field Guide to Holiday Candy & Confections*. All of these books feature a user-friendly format in which each recipe, in this case a cupcake, is presented on its own two-page spread. For each cupcake recipe you will find a Holiday (a suggested time to offer the cupcake), a Description (what you can expect to taste), Field Notes (where I give you tips and background information), and a Lifespan (which gives storage information and how long the cupcake stays fresh). At the end of many recipes are Cupcake Tips (where you will find any additional information about that cupcake that I thought would be helpful). You will also find symbols for special characteristics, as listed in the following chart:

quick to make

 cupcakes keep well

 fun to make with kids

 extra fancy

The main difference between this Field Guide and the three earlier ones is that in the beginning of this book you will find master recipes (pages 18–34) for cupcakes and frostings, from which all of the decorated cupcakes are created. Variations on these basics reside within the individual recipes themselves. Master these simple basic recipes and you can make any of the cupcakes in the book—and even mix and match them to come up with your own flavor and design ideas.

Ingredients

Here is a short list of frequently called for ingredients used in this book. If you start with high-quality ingredients, you'll get the best results.

BUTTER: Use fresh unsalted butter.

SUGAR: When a recipe calls for sugar, it means regular granulated sugar.

Light and dark brown sugar: These should be firmly packed when measuring.

Confectioners' sugar: This almost always needs sifting before measuring,

or at least a good whisking in a bowl to remove lumps.

Colored sugars: Colored sugars and edible glitters are used to decorate cupcakes and can be found in a variety of hues.

Sugar decorations: Whether they are tiny balls called nonpareils, or they are shaped like dots of confetti, tiny carrots, or spiders, look to cake-decorating supply sources for a variety of choices.

EGGS: Use eggs graded "large."

FLOUR: Use all-purpose flour. These recipes were tested with King Arthur Unbleached All-Purpose Flour.

LEAVENERS: Make sure your baking soda and baking powder are fresh. I use double-acting baking powder.

SALT: Use regular table salt; coarse salts measure differently.

MILK, CREAM CHEESE, AND SOUR CREAM: Use full-fat varieties.

HEAVY CREAM: Use cream labeled "heavy" as opposed to "whipping" for best results. The "heavy" has a higher butterfat content.

EXTRACTS: Use pure vanilla and almond extracts.

CITRUS ZESTS: Make sure to use only the colored part of the zest and not the bitter white pith underneath. Use a microplane zester for best results.

CHOCOLATE: Use the best quality chocolate you can find and afford. You can buy many good chocolates in specialty food stores and through mail-order (see Resources).

Bittersweet and semisweet chocolate: While these chocolates often can be used interchangeably, if I specify a particular chocolate, I suggest using it for best results. I enjoy using Scharffen Berger and Valrhona.

Milk chocolate: Use high-quality brands such as Michel Cluizel, Callebaut, and Valrhona.

White chocolate: Look for white chocolate that lists cocoa butter in the ingredients rather than palm oil or other oils. The cocoa butter will give it a natural chocolate flavor and aroma. I most often use Callebaut and Valrhona.

Chocolate coating or confectionery coating: This is a chocolate-like product that comes in white, milk, and dark varieties, but it does not contain any cocoa butter. Its fat content comes from various oils instead. It does not have the rich flavor of high-quality chocolate made with cocoa butter, but it is very easy to melt and use, and is fabulous for making Chocolate Plastic (page 111). Try Wilton's Candy Melts for that recipe.

COCOA POWDER: These recipes call for Dutch-processed cocoa powder, so check the label. It might say "Dutch," "Dutched," or "alkalized," but if it says "natural," that's the other kind (the wrong kind for these recipes). Dutch-processed cocoa powder is darker and has a more rounded flavor.

NUTS: Make sure nuts are fresh, with no rancid smell.

COCONUT: Unsweetened dried coconut is finely grated in texture; it can be found in natural foods stores. Sweetened flaked coconut has larger shreds and a sweeter taste, and it can be found in the supermarket, usually alongside the chocolate morsels.

SPICES: All of the spices called for in this book are ground; make sure they are fresh.

FOOD COLORS: I call for colored pastes, gels, liquids, and powders. See individual recipes for specific items required and information on where to purchase them.

GOLD LEAF AND GOLD AND SILVER POWDER: Believe it or not, you can eat gold leaf. Maybe not by the cupful, but little bits here and there are fine. You can buy it at art supply stores or through mail-order (see Resources). Just make sure to buy at least 22 karat for it to be safe enough to use with food. The silver and gold colored powders can be ordered through Beryl's Cake Decorating and Pastry Supplies (see Resources).

Equipment

CUPCAKE OR MUFFIN TINS: These terms can be used interchangeably. For our purposes, I'll refer to them as cupcake tins. I am referring, of course, to the tins that usually have 6 or 12 wells in which to pour batter and bake our little round

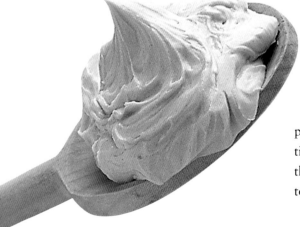

cakes. The problem is that while many may appear to be "standard" size (as opposed to mini or giant), there is variation from brand to brand. I use cupcake tins that hold ½ cup of water in each well if measured right to the brim. I tested these recipes with heavy-duty nonstick tins, such as those made by Wilton, which also happen to have nice broad rims that are easy to grab while moving tins in and out of the oven. You can also find tins with straight sides in the muffin wells, rather than the more traditional slanted sides, and they will give the cupcakes a different look. For the straight-sided look I use a brand called Gastroflex (see Resources), which is flexible and made of silicone. Silicone bakeware must be placed on a jelly-roll pan for support. Cupcakes baked in silicone often take longer to bake, as there is no metal to conduct the heat, so test carefully for doneness. For the recipes in this book in which I suggest using straight-sided pans, I do not use paper liners, as I want straight, smooth sides and the papers create ridges.

A couple of recipes use miniature cupcake tins. The batter for each standard-size cupcake will make about 4 miniature ones (and, of course, baking time will be shorter). Two recipes use a square-sided cupcake tin, which is sold exclusively by King Arthur Flour The Baker's Catalogue (see Resources). This tin has a slightly larger well than a standard cupcake tin.

PAPER LINERS: You may bake your batter directly in the cupcake tins, or you may use paper liners. In addition, some paper liners can even be used without tins. Every supermarket baking aisle will stock basic solid-color paper liners, usually in pastel shades, and these are fine. Sometimes you can find silver or gold foil liners that can be used with or without the tins. Their foil construction is stiff enough that you can place them directly on a jelly-roll pan. At baking supply stores, and through mail-order, the sky's the limit! You can get most any color that you like, as well as designs such as hearts for Valentine's Day, shamrocks for St. Patrick's Day, etc. There are also cupcake-sized panettone bread wrappers, which are deep, straight sided, and come in a subtle brown and beige pattern (and are almost 1 cup in volume). You will need those to make the Christmas Tree Cupcakes on page 104. I also use a darker brown paper type of liner that has deep, wide, fluted ridges, which give the cupcakes a sophisticated look. You will see a particular liner used in the photograph that accompanies each recipe, but feel free to pick and choose to your liking. Note that when using any kind of foil style, the cupcakes often bake a tad quicker.

PASTRY BAGS, COUPLER, AND TIPS: Some of these recipes require the use of a pastry bag and decorating tips. Where the directions call for a pastry bag and coupler and a specific tip, this means that the tip requires a coupler to be used. (A coupler is a plastic attachment that fits into the bag and allows you to change tips easily.) Where a coupler is not suggested, it is intended that you insert the tip, in this case a larger one, such as Wilton #2110 or Ateco #835, directly into the pastry bag. If you have the larger-style couplers, they can be used but are not necessary.

THERMOMETER: An accurate candy thermometer is not necessary for the Italian Meringue Buttercream (page 32) or the Fluffy Meringue Frosting (page 31), but it makes their preparation easier. You can find inexpensive candy thermometers in the supermarket.

MEASURING CUPS AND SPOONS: For dry ingredients, I use high-quality stainless steel cups that are sturdy enough not to dent (dents make for inaccurate measurements). The same goes for measuring spoons. For liquid measurements, I use

the standard Pyrex measuring cups available at most supermarkets and kitchenware stores. I use the dip-and-sweep method for measuring sugar and flour. Whisk flour first to aerate, then dip and sweep. For liquid measurements, use a cup similar to the amount you are measuring (in other words, do not use a 4-cup measuring cup to measure out ½ cup of liquid).

MIXER: I used a freestanding 5-quart KitchenAid mixer to test these recipes. If using a handheld mixer, the mixing times will be longer.

FOOD PROCESSOR: The recipes were tested with a KitchenAid 11-cup Ultra Power Food Processor.

MICROWAVE OVEN: It is hard to standardize recipes using microwave ovens, as different models may have different wattages. Always follow your manufacturer's directions for specific information. I use the microwave to melt dark chocolate and butter. Start by microwaving on 30 percent power for short periods of time.

JELLY-ROLL PANS: Many lighter-weight sheet-style pans are flimsy and can warp. These recipes were tested with heavy-weight aluminum rimmed sheet pans, which I refer to as jelly-roll pans.

Measuring Confectioners' Sugar
Many professional bakers like to weigh ingredients, as it is the most accurate way to determine amounts. However, this is not practical or possible for most home bakers, so recipes typically use volume measurements. I think that of all the commonly used baking ingredients, con-

fectioners' sugar is the most difficult to measure by volume, because depending on how you do it, your results will vary greatly. For these recipes, place confectioners' sugar straight from its box or bag into a mixing bowl. Whisk it around to remove lumps and to fluff it up a little bit. If lumps persist, then sift it. Now dip and sweep using the correct measuring cup. Any other way of measuring confectioners' sugar will give you amounts different than what I intend.

That said, the amounts of confectioners' sugar called for in the frosting recipes should be thought of as guidelines. Have some extra confectioners' sugar on hand in case you want or need to make the frostings a bit thicker and stiffer (as when piping out "grass," for instance).

Peeling and Toasting Nuts

HAZELNUTS: One technique will both skin and toast hazelnuts. Spread nuts in a single layer on a jelly-roll pan and toast in a 350°F oven until they begin to give off an aroma and the skins have turned dark brown and have split. This will take about 10 minutes. Shake the pan once or twice during toasting to encourage even browning. Remove from the oven and cool on a rack, then rub the nuts vigorously in clean kitchen towels. With a little elbow grease, the skins will come off. My

hazelnuts usually retain a tiny bit of skin on them; that's fine. Hazelnuts can be purchased peeled, at an added expense, but the time saved might be worth the expenditure.

WALNUTS AND PECANS: These do not need to be peeled. To toast, spread in a single layer on a jelly-roll pan and toast in a 350°F oven until fragrant and just beginning to color. This will take 5 to 10 minutes, depending on whether they are whole or in pieces. Shake the pan once or twice during toasting to encourage even browning.

Always cool nuts before chopping or grinding them. The oils, which will have been brought to the surface by the heat of the oven, must be reabsorbed or the nuts could turn greasy when chopped.

Making Cupcakes

This book is set up so that the master recipes for cakes and frostings are near the front of the book; the individual cupcake recipes combine these options and sometimes suggest variations, such as adding chopped dried fruit or nuts to a batter or adding flavor or color to a frosting.

Mastering any of the cake recipes is very easy. Two cautions: First, these are all so simple that every ingredient and every measurement really make a difference. Just two extra tablespoons of flour may throw off the balance. Second, cupcakes are very easy to overbake. I think overbaking is the number one downfall when it comes to making great cupcakes. They are small, so the surface area that is in contact with the tins is large and the baking time is short. If you test with a toothpick and there are crumbs clinging and you are not sure if they are done enough—in other words, if you are on the fence about whether they are done or not—remove them from the oven! There is residual heat from the pans, and with cupcakes it is better to err on this side of caution.

Most of the master cupcake recipes can be made up to two days before serving, and several of the frostings can be made ahead as well. Many of the finished cupcakes, on the other hand, are best eaten the day they are frosted and decorated, so in this case, bake the cupcake part ahead and then frost and decorate the day you intend to serve them. Specific tips are given within each recipe.

Liners vs. No Liners, and Peaked vs. Flat-Topped Cupcakes

You might think the decision to use liners is purely aesthetic, but it is much more than that. If you have time, conduct an experiment in which you line half of your cupcake wells with paper liners and leave the other half unlined. Same batter, same oven, same timing . . . you will see a big difference. Typically, cupcakes with liners bake up with a neater-looking dome on top, a gently rounded appearance to the top of the cupcake. Without liners, they can bake up very flat. (The exception is the brownie cupcake, which is always flat.) While the difference is dramatic, the choice might not be obvious. Review what the recipe is suggesting for décor. Sometimes you want a flatter surface, and sometimes a domed shape is helpful, useful, and very attractive. If you bake with liners and get a dome shape when what you need is a flat surface, you can always trim—but the other way around doesn't work! An exception is when glazing cupcakes with a poured fondant. In this case, I direct you to make very short cupcakes baked with liners so that the poured fondant creates a finished surface that's level with the top of the liners. Generally, if you do not use paper liners, you will want to spray the cupcake wells with nonstick cooking spray to allow for easy removal.

Filling the Tins

These recipes, unless otherwise stated, use a standard-size cupcake tin in which each well holds ½ cup of water. In general, you want to fill the tins about two-thirds to three-quarters of the way full. This gives you a very large, voluptuous cupcake. I find that filling the wells is most easily accomplished by using a spring-loaded ice cream scoop. After you bake a particular batter in your particular tins, make a note as to how high you filled them, and adjust for future batches if necessary.

There are two exceptions to these guidelines for filling the tins. Brownie batter does not rise very much—maybe ¼ inch—and doesn't develop a dome at all. So fill this batter almost to the level that you want it after baking. Occasionally the brownie batter will sink a bit in the center after cooling. Simply fill with icing, as desired.

On the other hand, when the recipe calls for glazing with poured fondant, it is best to have a shorter, shallower cupcake. After baking, you want the cupcake top to be beneath the top level of the paper liner. This way you can use the liner to hold the liquid fondant in place when it is poured over the cupcake. Individual recipes using fondant provide more specific information about this technique.

How to Make Perfect Cupcakes

- Read every recipe through before starting and follow the instructions to the letter.
- Use the ingredients called for (for instance, do not substitute jumbo eggs for large eggs).
- Take time to measure accurately with the proper tools.
- Use time cues and visual cues, when given, for best results.
- Do not overbake! Most cupcakes are ready when moist crumbs still cling to a wooden toothpick.
- Most cupcakes taste best when eaten the same day they are decorated.
- Relax and enjoy the cupcake-making process!

For individual recipes where I specify what tins you need and how many wells to fill, it is because the number of cupcakes differs from the basic recipe you are using.

In some of the recipes you will end up with empty wells because of the number of cupcakes in that particular recipe. These cupcakes will often bake a bit faster than if all the wells were filled. My mother always told me to partially fill empty wells with water to prevent damage to the tins and to encourage even baking. You may do this if you like, but I have not found it to make a big difference.

Testing for Doneness
The easiest mistake to make when baking cupcakes is to overbake them. They simply dry out too easily. All of the recipes suggest doneness when there are still crumbs clinging when tested with a toothpick. Notice I said toothpick, as in wooden toothpick. A wooden skewer is fine too. My point is that I find metal testers give different results. They don't really allow crumbs to cling, and so I do not recommend their use. The brownie cupcakes will show many moist crumbs when they are done—more than most, so take heed.

Storing Cupcakes

Most of these cupcakes should be stored at room temperature. Exceptions are explained in specific recipes. In general, I like to use airtight plastic containers that are deep enough to hold one layer of frosted decorated cupcakes. The cover should fit without crushing the frosting or decorations. Simply place the cupcakes side by side, snap on the lid, and take care to store the container on a level surface.

If you do not use paper liners, there is a chance that the sides of the cupcakes will stick together. You may separate rows with strips of parchment paper, cut to fit.

There are two storage solutions available that are made specifically for cupcakes. One is the Ultimate 3-in-1 Caddy from Wilton. It has circular ridges to hold individual cupcakes in place and will hold up to a dozen standard-size cupcakes under a snap-on airtight cover. But if you just want to pack one cupcake for your child to take to school—or you want to take one to work—look to King Arthur Flour The Baker's Catalogue (see Resources) for the Cup-a-Cake. It will hold one frosted cupcake perfectly!

Making Cupcakes with Kids

Cupcakes are all-around very kid friendly, and there are many ways to involve kids in the process. Certainly with many of the measuring aspects, there is room for them to help. Younger children can place liners in tins and scoop batter into them. Probably the best way kids can help is with the decorations. Some decorations are as easy as sprinkling something on top, which can be accomplished by even the youngest baker. Other décor ideas are a little more precise, like piping a specific shape on top of the cupcake, which slightly older kids can do. Some of the recipes do require a certain amount of skillfulness, such as making chocolate roses, and these would be best handled by an older child with an artsy-craftsy bent. As always, read the recipe thoroughly and make wise decisions. We don't want any kids getting discouraged about baking by a task that is beyond their skill or dexterity!

The
Master Recipes

White Cupcakes

This is a simple, moist white cake that can be varied endlessly. The cupcakes will keep for 2 days at room temperature in an airtight container or for 1 week frozen in an airtight container.

Yield: *12 cupcakes*

INGREDIENTS

- 12 paper liners
- 1¾ cups all-purpose flour
- 2 teaspoons baking powder
- ¼ teaspoon salt
- 3 large egg whites
- ¾ cup milk, at room temperature
- ½ cup (1 stick) unsalted butter, at room temperature, cut into small pieces
- ¾ cup sugar
- 1 teaspoon vanilla extract

DIRECTIONS

1. Preheat oven to 350°F. Place paper liners in all wells of one 12-cup cupcake tin.

2. Whisk flour, baking powder, and salt together in a small bowl to aerate and combine; set aside.

3. Whisk egg whites and milk together in a small bowl to combine; set aside.

4. In a large bowl with an electric mixer on medium-high speed, beat butter until creamy, about 2 minutes. Add sugar gradually, beating until light and fluffy, about 3 minutes, scraping down the bowl once or twice. Beat in vanilla extract. Add the flour mixture in 4 additions, alternately with the egg white–milk mixture. Begin and end with the flour mixture, and beat briefly until smooth on low-medium speed after each addition.

5. Divide batter evenly among cupcake wells. Bake for about 20 minutes, or until edges turn light golden brown; a toothpick inserted in the center will show a few moist crumbs.

6. Cool pan on rack for 5 minutes, then remove cupcakes to a cooling rack to cool completely.

Yellow Cupcakes

This is a classic moist yellow cake in a mini form. The cupcakes will keep for 2 days at room temperature in an airtight container or for 1 week frozen in an airtight container.

Yield: *12 cupcakes*

INGREDIENTS

12 paper liners
1½ cups all-purpose flour
1½ teaspoons baking
  powder
¼ teaspoon salt
½ cup (1 stick) unsalted
  butter, at room
  temperature, cut into
  small pieces
¾ cup sugar
1½ teaspoons vanilla
  extract
2 large eggs
½ cup milk, at room
  temperature

DIRECTIONS

1. Preheat oven to 350°F. Place paper liners in all wells of one 12-cup cupcake tin.

2. Whisk flour, baking powder, and salt together in a small bowl to aerate and combine; set aside.

3. In a large bowl with an electric mixer on medium-high speed, beat butter until creamy, about 2 minutes. Add sugar gradually, beating until light and fluffy, about 3 minutes, scraping down the bowl once or twice. Beat in vanilla extract. Beat in eggs one at a time, scraping down after each addition, allowing each egg to be absorbed before continuing. Add the flour mixture in 4 additions, alternately with the milk. Begin and end with the flour mixture, and beat briefly until smooth on low-medium speed after each addition.

4. Divide batter evenly among cupcake wells. Bake for about 18 minutes, or until a toothpick inserted in the center shows a few moist crumbs. The center should also spring back when lightly pressed. The cupcakes might color a bit around the edges, but they will not brown.

5. Cool pan on rack for 5 minutes, then remove cupcakes to a cooling rack to cool completely.

Variation
To make Marbled Cupcakes, melt 1 ounce unsweetened chocolate and allow to cool briefly. Divide batter in half and fold melted chocolate into one half. Divide yellow batter evenly among cupcake wells, then divide chocolate batter evenly among cupcake wells. The batter is thick, but as best as you can, use a wooden chopstick or a butter knife to marble the two batters together. Bake as directed.

Chocolate Cupcakes

Look no further for dark, moist, classic chocolate cupcakes. The cupcakes will keep for 2 days at room temperature in an airtight container or for 1 week frozen in an airtight container.

Yield: *18 cupcakes*

INGREDIENTS

18 paper liners
1½ cups all-purpose flour
½ cup Dutch-processed cocoa powder
¾ teaspoon baking soda
¼ teaspoon salt
½ cup (1 stick) unsalted butter, at room temperature, cut into small pieces
1⅓ cups sugar
1 teaspoon vanilla extract
2 large eggs
1 cup milk, at room temperature

DIRECTIONS

1. Preheat oven to 350°F. Place paper liners in all wells of one 12-cup and one 6-cup cupcake tin.

2. Whisk flour, cocoa powder, baking soda, and salt together in a small bowl to aerate and combine; set aside.

3. In a large bowl with an electric mixer on medium-high speed, beat butter until creamy, about 2 minutes. Add sugar gradually, beating until light and fluffy, about 3 minutes, scraping down the bowl once or twice. Beat in vanilla extract. Beat in eggs one at a time, scraping down after each addition, allowing each egg to be absorbed before continuing. Add the flour mixture in 4 additions, alternately with the milk. Begin and end with the flour mixture, and beat briefly until smooth on low-medium speed after each addition.

4. Divide batter evenly among cupcake wells. Bake for about 22 minutes, or until a toothpick inserted in the center shows a few moist crumbs.

5. Cool pans on racks for 5 minutes, then remove cupcakes to cooling racks to cool completely.

Pound Cake Cupcakes

Pound cake is rich and buttery and works well for individual cupcakes. These form a peak during baking, which can be sliced and leveled off before icing and decorating, if desired. The cupcakes will keep for 2 days at room temperature in an airtight container or for 1 week frozen in an airtight container.

Yield: *18 cupcakes*

INGREDIENTS

18 paper liners
2¼ cups all-purpose flour
1 teaspoon baking powder
¼ teaspoon salt
1½ cups (3 sticks)
  unsalted butter, at room
  temperature, cut into
  small pieces
1½ cups sugar
1 tablespoon vanilla extract
6 large eggs

DIRECTIONS

1. Preheat oven to 325°F. Place paper liners in all wells of one 12-cup and one 6-cup cupcake tin.

2. Whisk flour, baking powder, and salt together in a small bowl to aerate and combine; set aside.

3. In a large bowl with an electric mixer on medium-high speed, beat butter until creamy, about 4 minutes. Add sugar gradually, beating until light and fluffy, about 4 minutes, scraping down the bowl once or twice. Beat in vanilla extract. Beat in eggs one at a time, scraping down after each addition, allowing each egg to be absorbed before continuing. Add the flour mixture in 4 additions, beating just until smooth on low-medium speed after each addition.

4. Divide batter evenly among cupcake wells. Bake for about 22 minutes, or until a toothpick inserted in the center shows a few moist crumbs.

5. Cool pans on racks for 5 minutes, then remove cupcakes to cooling racks to cool completely.

Crumb Cake Cupcakes

Sour cream makes a very moist coffeecake, and this recipe works wonderfully with the addition of fruit or nuts or just as a plain spiced version. If you use frozen berries, there is no need to defrost them before adding them to the batter. If you leave out the fruit and nuts entirely, you will get about a dozen cupcakes. You can also use a combination

INGREDIENTS

Streusel:

½ cup (1 stick) unsalted butter, melted

⅔ cup sugar

2 teaspoons ground cinnamon

½ teaspoon vanilla extract

Pinch of salt

1¼ cups all-purpose flour

Cupcakes:

18 paper liners

2 cups all-purpose flour

1 teaspoon baking powder

½ teaspoon baking soda

Pinch of salt

½ cup (1 stick) unsalted butter, at room temperature, cut into small pieces

¾ cup plus 2 tablespoons sugar

2 teaspoons vanilla extract

¼ teaspoon almond extract

2 large eggs

1 cup sour cream

1½ cups fresh or frozen blueberries or raspberries *or* 1½ cups nuts, toasted (see page 13) and finely chopped (try walnuts, pecans, and/or almonds)

DIRECTIONS

1. To make the streusel, in a large bowl, stir together melted butter, sugar, cinnamon, vanilla extract, and salt until well combined. Stir in flour until smooth. Mixture should clump and form "crumbs" when squeezed between fingertips. Set aside.

2. To make the cupcakes, preheat oven to 350°F. Place paper liners in all wells of one 12-cup and one 6-cup cupcake tin.

3. Whisk flour, baking powder, baking soda, and salt together in a small bowl to aerate and combine; set aside.

4. In a large bowl with an electric mixer on medium-high speed, beat butter until creamy, about 2 minutes. Add sugar gradually, beating until light and fluffy, about 3 minutes, scraping down the bowl once or twice. Beat in extracts. Beat in eggs one at a time, scraping down after each addition, allowing each egg to be absorbed before continuing. Add the flour mixture in 4 additions, alternately with the sour cream. Begin and end with the flour mixture, stopping when there are still a few streaks of flour. Fold in the fruit and/or nuts, if using, until just combined.

of fruit and nuts totaling 1½ cups. The cupcakes will keep for 2 days at room temperature in an airtight container.

Yield: *18 cupcakes*

5. Divide batter evenly among cupcake wells. Place a generous amount of streusel on top of each cupcake, using your fingers to compress it into crumbs and to scatter it evenly. Bake for about 22 minutes, or until a toothpick inserted in the center shows a few moist crumbs.

6. Cool pans on racks for 5 minutes, then remove cupcakes to cooling racks to cool completely.

Cupcake Tips

The baking time will depend on whether you are using fresh fruit, frozen fruit, or none at all. If you leave out the fruit, begin checking for doneness after 18 minutes have elapsed.

Carrot Cake Cupcakes

This perennial favorite cake flavor works wonderfully for cupcakes. Make sure to use a light-flavored oil, such as canola or vegetable oil. I like a small-size shred for the carrots, which can be accomplished by using the small holes on a box grater or by using the small-size shredding disc on a food processor. You may halve this recipe for an even dozen, but they freeze very well (the oil keeps them soft and moist), so why not make a full batch? No need to use a mixer for this recipe; these cupcakes are quickly made with a whisk. The cupcakes will keep for 2 days at room temperature in an airtight container or for 1 week frozen in an airtight container.

Yield: *24 cupcakes*

INGREDIENTS

- 24 paper liners
- 2 cups all-purpose flour
- 1½ teaspoons baking powder
- 1½ teaspoons baking soda
- 2 teaspoons ground cinnamon
- 1 teaspoon ground ginger
- ¼ teaspoon ground nutmeg
- Pinch of salt
- ¾ cup canola oil or vegetable oil
- ¾ cup granulated sugar
- ¾ cup firmly packed dark brown sugar
- 2 teaspoons vanilla extract
- 4 large eggs
- 2 cups grated carrots (from about 3 large carrots)
- 1¼ cups walnut halves, toasted (see page 13) and finely chopped
- 1 cup dark raisins

DIRECTIONS

1. Preheat oven to 350°F. Place paper liners in all wells of two 12-cup cupcake tins.

2. Whisk flour, baking powder, baking soda, spices, and salt together in a small bowl to aerate and combine; set aside.

3. In a large bowl whisk together oil, granulated sugar, and brown sugar until well blended, about 1 minute. Whisk in vanilla extract, then whisk in eggs one at a time, allowing each egg to be absorbed before continuing. Whisk in carrots. Stir in dry mixture until almost completely blended. Add nuts and raisins and stir just until blended. (An extra-large rubber spatula works great here.)

4. Divide batter evenly among cupcake wells. Bake for about 18 minutes, or until a toothpick inserted in the center shows a few moist crumbs.

5. Cool pans on racks for 5 minutes, then remove cupcakes to cooling racks to cool completely.

Brownie Cupcakes

This is a classic brownie batter baked in a cupcake shape. These cupcakes are very rich and fudgy and bake up with a flat top. The cupcakes will keep for 2 days at room temperature in an airtight container or for 1 week frozen in an airtight container.

Yield: *18 cupcakes*

INGREDIENTS

18 paper liners
8 ounces semisweet or bittersweet chocolate, finely chopped
1 cup (2 sticks) unsalted butter, at room temperature, cut into pieces
2 cups firmly packed light brown sugar
4 large eggs
2 teaspoons vanilla extract
¼ teaspoon salt
1 cup all-purpose flour
¾ cup pecan halves (optional), toasted (see page 13) and finely chopped

DIRECTIONS

1. Preheat oven to 350°F. Place paper liners in all wells of one 12-cup and one 6-cup cupcake tin.

2. Melt chocolate and butter together in top of large double boiler or in large bowl in microwave; stir until smooth and combined, then cool to lukewarm.

3. Whisk in brown sugar until well blended. Then whisk in eggs one at a time, allowing each one to become absorbed before adding next one. Whisk in vanilla extract and salt. Add flour and nuts, if using, at the same time and fold in until no streaks of flour remain.

4. Divide batter evenly among cupcake wells. Bake for about 25 minutes, or until a toothpick inserted in the center shows many moist crumbs. The tops will be dry and crackled in appearance and slightly puffed.

5. Cool pans on racks for 5 minutes, then remove cupcakes to cooling racks to cool completely.

Cupcake Tips

With brownies it is hard to gauge doneness—they will seem wet in the center as compared to the other cupcakes in the book—but they are done! You may leave out the nuts, of course, or substitute mini chocolate chips, or white chocolate chips, or chopped cherries, or whatever add-in you like.

Classic Confectioners' Sugar Frosting

This is very easy to make and is the go-to frosting for many cupcake bakers. This recipe is for a basic vanilla version; flavor variations appear in individual recipes. Make sure to measure your confectioners' sugar carefully—see page 12 for tips. The frosting is best if used immediately, but it may be refrigerated in an airtight container for up to 4 days.

Yield: *about 3 cups*

INGREDIENTS

- ½ cup (1 stick) unsalted butter, at room temperature, cut into small pieces
- 4 cups confectioners' sugar, plus an additional ½ cup if necessary, whisked before measuring
- ¼ cup milk, at room temperature
- 1 teaspoon vanilla extract

DIRECTIONS

1. In a large bowl with an electric mixer on medium-high speed, beat butter until creamy, about 2 minutes. Add 1 cup confectioners' sugar gradually, beating until light and fluffy, about 3 minutes, scraping down the bowl once or twice. Add 1 more cup of sugar and about half of the milk and beat until smooth and creamy. Add 1 more cup of sugar and remaining milk, and beat well, scraping down sides of the bowl. Add remaining 1 cup of sugar and vanilla extract and beat on high speed until very light and creamy, about 5 minutes. Assess texture. If it is too soft, add a portion or all of the remaining ½ cup of sugar.

2. At this point you can continue beating the frosting, if you like, which will make it lighter, creamier, and a little airier. You want it to be as smooth as possible. Frosting is ready to use. (Bring to room temperature and rebeat after storing.)

Cupcake Tips

For certain applications, such as when making "grass" for Easter Basket Cupcakes (page 52), you will need a thicker frosting. Just add additional confectioners' sugar until the desired texture is reached.

Fudge Frosting

In terms of flavor and thickness, this chocolate frosting is in the middle; the Ganache Glaze and Frosting on page 28 is darker and richer, and the chocolate version of the Italian Meringue Buttercream on page 32 is lighter. The frosting is best if used immediately, but it may be refrigerated in an airtight container for up to 4 days.

Yield: *about 2 cups*

INGREDIENTS

¼ cup (½ stick) unsalted butter, at room temperature, cut into small pieces

4 cups confectioners' sugar, plus an additional ½ cup if necessary, whisked before measuring

⅓ cup milk, at room temperature

1 teaspoon vanilla extract

3 ounces unsweetened chocolate, melted and slightly cooled

DIRECTIONS

1. In a large bowl with an electric mixer on medium-high speed, beat butter until creamy, about 2 minutes. Add 1 cup sugar gradually, beating until light and fluffy, about 3 minutes, scraping down the bowl once or twice. Add remaining 3 cups sugar and the milk and beat on high speed until smooth and creamy. Add vanilla extract and melted chocolate and beat until combined.

2. If the chocolate is too warm, the frosting might be too soft to hold peaks. Just keep beating until it is thick enough to spread. Assess texture. If it is too soft, add a portion or all of the remaining ½ cup of sugar. Frosting is ready to use. (Bring to room temperature and rebeat after storing.)

Cupcake Tips

If the frosting remains too soft, it is probably because the chocolate was too warm. If beating it does not thicken it, place the bowl over ice and stir occasionally until thickened. Or, if it is already chilled and still seems too soft, simply add more confectioners' sugar.

Ganache Glaze and Frosting

This ganache is the darkest, richest, most chocolatey icing in the book. If you use it right away, while it is liquid, you can coat the tops of cupcakes with it for a smooth, shiny, glazed appearance. If you let it rest overnight at a cool room temperature (or refrigerate it briefly), you can place it in a pastry bag fitted with a decorating tip and pipe rosettes, big swirls, or small bead shapes, or even use it for writing or other decorative details. The ganache will keep for 1 week refrigerated in an airtight container or for 1 month frozen in an airtight container.

Yield: *1½ cups glaze or frosting*

INGREDIENTS

⅔ cup heavy cream
10 ounces semisweet or bittersweet chocolate, finely chopped

DIRECTIONS

1. Place cream in a medium-large saucepan and bring to a boil over medium heat.

2. Remove from the heat and immediately sprinkle chocolate into cream. Cover and allow to sit for 5 minutes. The heat of the cream should melt the chocolate. Gently stir the ganache until smooth. If the chocolate is not melting, place over very low heat, stirring often, until melted, taking care not to burn the chocolate.

3. The ganache is ready to use. You may dip the tops of cupcakes upside down into the ganache, gently swirling them around, before flipping upright. Or you may apply liquid ganache with a spoon directly onto the tops of the cupcakes. Alternatively, you may allow the ganache to firm up overnight at room temperature or until it is a spreadable consistency (between mayonnaise and peanut butter). At this point you may apply it with an icing spatula or place in a pastry bag with decorating tip of choice. If it becomes too firm, or if you would like to return it to a liquid state, simply place over a warm burner or microwave briefly.

Cupcake Tips

If you are using this as a fluid glaze and it seems thick, just add a little extra cream, a teaspoon at a time, until you reach the desired texture. Also, upon reheating, if the texture of the ganache is not smooth, dribble in a tiny bit of cold heavy cream and whisk together until smooth. Keep in mind that different chocolates will produce different textures with this recipe, as well as different flavors.

Cream Cheese Frosting

This frosting is not just for carrot cake. It is rich and creamy and works great with other cupcake recipes as well. The frosting is best if used immediately, but it may be refrigerated in an airtight container for up to 4 days.

Yield: *about 4 cups*

INGREDIENTS

- 10 tablespoons (1 stick plus 2 tablespoons) unsalted butter, at room temperature, cut into small pieces
- 1¼ pounds cream cheese, at room temperature
- 2½ teaspoons vanilla extract
- 3½ cups confectioners' sugar, whisked before measuring

DIRECTIONS

In a large bowl with an electric mixer on medium-high speed, beat butter, cream cheese, and vanilla extract until creamy, about 3 minutes. Add sugar gradually, beating until light and fluffy, about 3 minutes, scraping down the bowl once or twice. Frosting is now ready to use. (Rebeat after storing.)

Whipped Cream Frosting

Confectioners' sugar has a bit of cornstarch added to it to help prevent clumping. By using confectioners' sugar as the sweetener for this recipe, the tiny bit of cornstarch helps stabilize the finished whipped cream. This frosting is best if used immediately.

Yield: *about 2¼ cups*

INGREDIENTS

- 1½ cups heavy cream
- 3 tablespoons confectioners' sugar
- ¼ teaspoon vanilla extract

DIRECTIONS

1. In a large, chilled bowl with an electric mixer on medium-high speed, beat cream until it begins to thicken. Add sugar and vanilla extract and beat until soft peaks form.

2. For some recipes, you can use the frosting at this point; for others, continue to whip until stiffer peaks form, but do not overwhip. If it shows clumps and lumps, it is overwhipped. Simply stir in some additional liquid cream to smooth it out. Frosting is ready to use.

Fluffy Meringue Frosting

If you have been looking for a fat-free vanilla frosting, this is it! It is bright white and very sweet and has a marshmallow quality to it. You might notice that the recipe is similar to the Italian Meringue Buttercream (page 32), but without the butter. Again, though a candy thermometer is not necessary, it is helpful. Make sure that no grease comes in contact with the frosting, or the meringue will deflate and it will be ruined. This frosting must be used immediately.

Yield: *about 4½ cups*

INGREDIENTS

- ½ cup plus scant 2 tablespoons sugar
- 3 tablespoons water
- 3 large egg whites, at room temperature
- Heaping ¼ teaspoon cream of tartar
- Generous ¼ teaspoon vanilla extract

DIRECTIONS

1. Place ½ cup of sugar and the water in a small pot. Stir to wet sugar. Bring to a boil over medium-high heat, swirling pan occasionally. Dip pastry brush in cold water and wash down sugar crystals from the sides of the pot once or twice. Turn down heat to simmer gently.

2. Meanwhile, place the egg whites into a clean, grease-free mixing bowl and whip until frothy on low speed using balloon whip attachment to standing mixer. Add cream of tartar and turn speed up to medium-high. When soft peaks form, add remaining 2 tablespoons sugar gradually. Continue whipping until stiff, glossy peaks form.

3. Bring the sugar-water mixture to a rapid boil and cook until it reaches 248° to 250°F. As syrup cooks look for visual clues to assess temperature. It starts out thin with many small bubbles over the surface. The water will begin to evaporate and the mixture will become thicker. The bubbles get larger and sticky and pop more slowly. At this point the syrup looks thickened, but it has not begun to color. If you drop a bit of the syrup into a glass of cold water it will form into a ball. This is the firm-ball stage, and the syrup is ready.

4. Pour a thin, steady stream over meringue, without pouring any on the rotating whip or the sides of the bowl. Whip meringue on high speed until cool to the touch. Beat in vanilla. Frosting is ready to use.

31

Italian Meringue Buttercream

This is an ultra-smooth, not-too-sweet buttercream best used for fancier cupcakes. It may be flavored endlessly, adding anything from chocolate (any kind) to liqueurs, pureed fruits, juices, or even coffee. A stand mixer is best for this recipe, as it will have to beat for quite a while. Although I give visual cues for the sugar syrup, a candy thermometer eliminates uncertainty. It is vitally important that any cupcake frosted with this buttercream be served at room temperature. There is

INGREDIENTS

Scant ⅔ cup plus 3
  tablespoons sugar
¼ cup water
4 large egg whites, at room
  temperature
½ teaspoon cream of tartar
1½ cups (3 sticks)
  unsalted butter, at room
  temperature, cut into
  small pieces

DIRECTIONS

1. Place ⅔ cup sugar and the water in a small pot. Stir to wet sugar. Bring to a boil over medium-high heat, swirling pan occasionally. Dip pastry brush in cold water and wash down sugar crystals from the sides of the pot once or twice. Turn down heat to simmer gently.

2. Place the egg whites in a clean, grease-free mixing bowl and whip until frothy on low speed using balloon whip attachment to standing mixer. Add cream of tartar and turn speed to medium-high. When soft peaks form, add remaining 3 tablespoons sugar gradually. Continue whipping until stiff, glossy peaks form. (This is the meringue part of the buttercream, and the frosting may be used at this point for a low-fat, marshmallow-like frosting; it must be used immediately.)

3. Bring the sugar-water mixture to a rapid boil and cook until it reaches 248° to 250°F. As syrup cooks, look for visual clues to assess temperature. It starts out thin with many small bubbles over the surface. The water will begin to evaporate and the mixture will become thicker. The bubbles get larger and sticky and pop more slowly. At this point the syrup looks thickened, but it has not begun to color. If you drop a bit of the syrup into a glass of cold water it will form into a ball. This is the firm-ball stage, and the syrup is ready.

4. Pour a thin, steady stream over meringue, without pouring any on the rotating whip or the sides of the

so much butter in this recipe that it is quite firm when chilled. Not only will the texture be unpleasant, but the flavor will be muted. The buttercream will keep for 1 week refrigerated in an airtight container or for 1 month frozen in an airtight container. (If frozen, defrost it in the refrigerator overnight and bring it to warm room temperature before rebeating. I highly suggest warming it in the microwave before rebeating.)

Yield: *about 3½ cups*

bowl. Whip meringue on high speed until cool. When the bowl is no longer warm, stop the machine and touch the surface of the meringue with your finger to check that it is cooled. With mixer on medium speed, add the butter, a couple of table-spoons at a time. Keep beating until the butter-cream is completely smooth. Your buttercream is ready to use. Any flavorings may be added at this point; variations are given in individual recipes. (Rebeat after storing.)

Cupcake Tips

Temperature is everything with this buttercream. If ingredients are warm or hot when combined, it will become soupy and loose. If they are cold, the mixture will be lumpy and too firm. If you do end up with a loose buttercream, chill it by placing the bottom of the bowl in a larger bowl filled with ice water for a few minutes before proceeding. If the mixture is too cold and stiff, just keep whipping. It will smooth out. Or, if you prefer, aim a hot hair dryer at the outside of the bowl; it will warm up the buttercream quickly. You may also place a cup of buttercream in the microwave for a few seconds, then add it back to the larger amount to bring batch to a warmer temperature and smoother texture.

Poured Fondant Glaze

This is a simple poured glaze that firms to a satiny finish. It starts out as a white icing, but can easily be turned into a rich chocolatey icing by following the last step below. In fact, it is very easy to divide the recipe in half and make both flavors at once. See pages 14–15 for a brief description of fondant glazing techniques. Individual recipes give more thorough descriptions of how to use this glaze. This glaze is best if used immediately, but may be stored at room temperature in an airtight container for up to 4 days.

Yield: *about 2 cups*

INGREDIENTS

½ cup water
¼ cup light corn syrup
5 cups confectioners' sugar, whisked before measuring
4 ounces unsweetened chocolate, finely chopped (for chocolate version)

DIRECTIONS

1. Place water and corn syrup in a medium-size sauce-pan, stir to combine, and bring to a boil over medium-high heat.

2. Remove from heat and whisk in confectioners' sugar, 1 cup at a time, until fondant is completely smooth, creamy white, and lump free. Fondant is ready to use in this liquid form, or you can follow the next step to turn it into chocolate fondant.

3. For chocolate fondant, stir in chopped chocolate. Allow to stand for a few minutes to allow residual heat to melt chocolate. If it isn't melting, or mixture is too thick, place over very low heat and gently stir until melted and smooth. Fondant is ready to use. The temperature might have to be adjusted. If the fondant glaze is too warm, it will be too runny. If it is too cool, a crust will form. Cool it just enough so that it falls from a spoon slowly, but is still fluid. (Rewarm after storing until it reaches desired consistency.)

Cupcake Tips

To make both flavors at once, divide the fondant into 2 bowls at the end of step 2. Stir 2 ounces of unsweetened chocolate into one of the bowls. If the chocolate version becomes too thick, thin it by whisking in ½ teaspoon of hot water at a time until the desired consistency is reached.

The
Field Guide

"Champagne" Cupcakes

🧁 **HOLIDAY** *New Year's Eve*

🧁 **DESCRIPTION** *White or yellow cupcakes are topped with a poured white fondant glaze. After the fondant firms up, small champagne glasses are piped on top; edible glitter and very pearly dragées form "champagne bubbles."*

🧁 **FIELD NOTES** *While I use champagne flutes to drink my champagne, I thought the saucer-style champagne glass was more visually appropriate for these cupcakes. The Wilton Icing Writer makes the process of piping the champagne glasses very quick and easy. You can find the tiny dragées at Beryl's (see Resources).*

🧁 **LIFESPAN** *Cupcakes may be baked 2 days ahead; frosted cupcakes are best served the same day. Store at room temperature in airtight container.*

Yield: *23 festive cupcakes*

INGREDIENTS

23 paper liners
1 batch batter from White Cupcakes (page 18) or Yellow Cupcakes (page 19)
1 batch Poured Fondant Glaze (page 34)
Liqueur of your choice, such as Grand Marnier or Kahlúa

Wilton Icing Writer in White
White edible glitter, such as Wilton Cake Sparkles
Tiny pearl dragées (about 3 millimeters in size)

DIRECTIONS

1. Preheat oven to 350°. Place paper liners in 23 wells of two 12-cup cupcake tins.

2. Divide batter evenly among paper liners. The liners will be only one-third full (so there is headroom for the poured glaze later on). Bake for about 16 minutes, or until a toothpick inserted in center shows a few moist crumbs. Cool pans on racks for 5 minutes, then remove cupcakes to cooling racks to cool completely.

3. Place cupcakes on jelly-roll pan. Pierce each several times with a bamboo skewer. Sprinkle liqueur, straight out of the bottle, on each one. The amount used will depend on strength of liqueur and potency desired!

4. Use a teaspoon to pour the fluid fondant in the center of each cupcake, applying enough so that it spreads out on its own and flows to the edges of the liners. Make sure to cover cake completely while fondant is still fluid. Allow to set and dry, which will take just a few minutes. If you can still see the cake, or if the center of the cupcake is peaked, simply glaze a second time, adding enough fondant to create a smooth, flat, opaque surface.

5. While surface is still slightly moist, use Icing Writer to pipe outline of a champagne glass shape, then fill in with Icing Writer. Sprinkle glitter and dragées above cup to mimic champagne bubbles (as in photograph). Allow to set and dry. Cupcakes are now ready to serve.

Cupcake Tips

The liqueur is optional, of course. If you are expecting kids at your party, make some without. Just make theirs in a different color paper liner to keep track.

Chocolate-Covered Cherry Cupcakes

🍒 **HOLIDAY** *New Year's Eve*

🍒 **DESCRIPTION** *Buried inside these elegant cupcakes is a chocolate-covered cherry. Rich chocolate buttercream adorns the top and another chocolate-covered cherry crowns them. They are a chocolate-and-cherry lover's dream!*

🍒 **FIELD NOTES** *According to some Internet sources, January 3 is Chocolate-Covered Cherry Day. This is of particular interest to me, as January 3 is my twins' birthday—and we all love chocolates and cherries together. The results will largely depend on the quality of chocolate-covered cherries you can find. Most common are chocolate-covered maraschino cherries. If possible, search out a high-end chocolate shop that makes their own and uses Morello cherries or a similarly less sweet cherry.*

🍒 **LIFESPAN** *Cupcakes may be baked 2 days ahead; frosted cupcakes are best served the same day. Store refrigerated in airtight container.*

Yield: *18 cupcakes with a hidden surprise*

 INGREDIENTS

18 red or pink paper liners
1 batch batter from Chocolate Cupcakes
   (page 20)
36 chocolate-covered cherries
1 batch Italian Meringue Buttercream
   (page 32)

7 ounces bittersweet chocolate, melted
   and slightly cooled
Pastry bag
Large star tip

DIRECTIONS

1. Preheat oven to 350°F. Place paper liners in all wells of one 12-cup and one 6-cup cupcake tin. Divide batter among liners. Press a chocolate-covered cherry (stem removed, if necessary) into the center of each cupcake. Smooth batter over cherry with small offset spatula to cover completely.

2. Bake for about 22 minutes, or until a toothpick inserted into the cake portion of the cupcake shows a few moist crumbs. Cool pans on racks for 5 minutes, then remove cupcakes to cooling racks to cool completely.

3. Place the buttercream in a large mixing bowl and beat in the 7 ounces of cooled melted bittersweet chocolate. Using a pastry bag fitted with a large star tip, frost each cupcake with a large swirl on top. Top each cupcake with another chocolate-covered cherry. Cupcakes are now ready to serve. (You may refrigerate them for most of the day, but make sure to bring back to room temperature before serving.)

Cupcake Tips

You don't need cherries with stems attached, but if you can find them, they look great on top of the cupcake!

"Be Mine" Cupcakes

HOLIDAY *Valentine's Day*

DESCRIPTION *These cupcakes feature white cake batter with cinnamon red-hot candies folded into it for flavor, color, and crunch. The tops are glazed with pearly white or dark chocolate poured fondant. Personalized messages, such as "Be Mine" and "I ♥ You," can be written on top of each one with melted chocolate.*

FIELD NOTES *These are supposed to be like those little heart-shaped candies that have all sorts of short cute sayings on them. You can provide blank cupcakes at a party, and guests, whether adults or kids, can personalize them for their valentine. For the edible heart-shaped confetti, I like the large confetti that is about ½ inch across. These, and the pink nonpareils, can be ordered from Sweet Celebrations or New York Cake Supplies (see Resources). Use melted dark chocolate to write on the white fondant, or white chocolate to write on the dark chocolate fondant.*

LIFESPAN *Cupcakes may be baked 2 days ahead; frosted cupcakes are best served the same day. Store at room temperature in airtight container.*

Yield: *23 romantic cupcakes*

INGREDIENTS

23 red paper liners
½ cup cinnamon red-hot candies
1 batch batter from White Cupcakes (page 18) or Yellow Cupcakes (page 19)
1 batch Poured Fondant Glaze (white, chocolate, or both, page 34)

Red edible heart-shaped confetti (optional)
Pink nonpareils (optional)
2 ounces semisweet and/or white chocolate, melted
Parchment cone

DIRECTIONS

1. Preheat oven to 350°F. Place paper liners in 23 wells of two 12-cup cupcake tins.

2. Fold the cinnamon candies into the batter of your choice. Divide batter evenly among 23 paper liners. The liners will be only one-third full (so there is headroom for the poured glaze later on).

3. Bake for about 16 minutes, or until a toothpick inserted in center shows a few moist crumbs. Cool pans on racks for 5 minutes, then remove cupcakes to racks to cool completely.

4. Use a teaspoon to pour the fluid fondant over the center of each cupcake, applying enough so that it spreads out on its own and flows to the edges of the liners. Make sure to cover cake completely while fondant is still fluid. Allow to set and dry, which will take just a few minutes. If you can still see the cake, or if the center of the cupcake is peaked, simply glaze a second time, adding enough fondant to create a smooth, flat, opaque surface. While surface is still moist, arrange heart-shaped confetti around edge of cupcake, if desired, and/or sprinkle with pink nonpareils. Allow to set and dry.

5. Place melted chocolate in parchment cone. Snip a very small opening. Pipe sentiments on top of cupcakes as desired. Chill briefly to set chocolate. Cupcakes are now ready to serve.

Cupcake Tips

If you want to make a party out of this so folks can write their own notes, have melted chocolate in several parchment cones so everyone can get to work personalizing their edible valentines.

Red Velvet Cupcakes

🔴 **HOLIDAY** *Valentine's Day*

🔴 **DESCRIPTION** *Here the master chocolate cake batter is tinted with red food coloring to give it the classic reddish hue of red velvet cake. (Wilton Icing Color in Red Red is great for achieving this effect.) Topped with another classic, a fluffy white frosting, these cupcakes are just like that favorite retro dessert, in mini form. The crowning touch of a single pink "pearl" is optional, but very pretty.*

🔴 **FIELD NOTES** *The real history of red velvet cake is clouded. Did it come from the Waldorf-Astoria decades ago? Were the original "red" cakes not enhanced by dye, but simply reddish from a reaction between the cocoa and baking soda? Who knows, but I do know that the chocolate cake and white frosting combo is delicious. You can order the pink pearls from Beryl's or Sweet Celebrations (see Resources). These look very simple, and they are, and work perfectly when you need a restrained, elegant cupcake.*

🔴 **LIFESPAN** *Cupcakes may be baked 2 days ahead; frosted cupcakes are best served the same day. Store refrigerated in airtight container.*

Yield: *18 simple, elegant cupcakes*

 INGREDIENTS

18 red paper liners
Red food coloring
1 batch batter from Chocolate Cupcakes
(page 20)

1 batch Fluffy Meringue Frosting (page 31)
18 pink "pearls" (optional; try those at
least 6 millimeters in size)

DIRECTIONS

1. Preheat oven to 350°F. Place paper liners in all wells of one 12-cup and one 6-cup cupcake tin.

2. Beat enough food coloring into the cupcake batter until a pleasing reddish shade is reached. Divide batter evenly among cupcake wells. Bake for about 22 minutes, or until a toothpick inserted in the center shows a few moist crumbs. Cool pans on racks for 5 minutes, then remove cupcakes to cooling racks to cool completely.

3. Frost each cupcake generously using an icing spatula or a spoon. Top with a pink pearl, if using. Cupcakes are now ready to serve.

Heartfelt Cupcakes

🌸 **HOLIDAY** *Valentine's Day*

🌸 **DESCRIPTION** *These cupcakes are topped with heart-shaped butter cookies that have a small heart cut out from the center. When placed on top of the frosted cupcake, a bit of frosting pokes through the cutout—just enough to hold a sprinkling of edible red glitter. You may use any master cupcake recipe you like for this.*

🌸 **FIELD NOTES** *For this recipe you will be making cookies and cupcakes, but the cookies can be made several days ahead. You will need two heart-shaped cookie cutters: one about 1 inch across and one about 3 inches across.*

🌸 **LIFESPAN** *Cupcakes may be baked 2 days ahead; frosted cupcakes are best served the same day. Store at room temperature in airtight container if using Classic Confectioners' Sugar Frosting; store refrigerated in airtight container if using Italian Meringue Buttercream.*

Yield: *12 from-the-heart cupcakes*

INGREDIENTS

Cookies:

1¼ cups all-purpose flour
Pinch of salt
½ cup (1 stick) unsalted butter, at room temperature, cut into tablespoon-size pieces
½ cup sugar
½ teaspoon vanilla extract
1 large egg
3-inch heart-shaped cookie cutter
1-inch heart-shaped cookie cutter

1 batch Classic Confectioners' Sugar Frosting (page 26) or Italian Meringue Buttercream (page 32)
1½ teaspoons vanilla extract (if using Italian Meringue Buttercream)
12 cupcakes of your choice in paper liners of your choice
Red edible glitter, such as Wilton Cake Sparkles

DIRECTIONS

1. To make the cookies, whisk flour and salt together in a small bowl to aerate; set aside. In a large bowl with an electric mixer on medium-high speed, beat butter until creamy, about 2 minutes. Add sugar gradually, beating until light and fluffy, about 3 minutes, scraping down the bowl once or twice. Beat in vanilla extract. Beat in egg, then beat in the flour mixture in three additions. Form into a flat disc, wrap in plastic wrap, and refrigerate at least 2 hours, or until firm enough to roll. Dough may be refrigerated overnight. (You may freeze dough for up to 1 month; defrost in refrigerator overnight before proceeding.)

2. Preheat oven to 350°F. Line a jelly-roll pan with parchment paper.

3. Remove dough from refrigerator and roll out to ¼-inch thickness on floured surface; you may need to flour your rolling pin too. Cut out cookies with larger heart-shaped cutter. Transfer cookies to prepared pan, placing 2 inches apart. Once they are on the pan,

cut out small hearts from center of each cookie. (You can reroll this extra dough, if you like, to make more cookies).

4. Bake for about 10 minutes, or until edges have just begun to color; they should stay fairly pale. Slide parchment onto racks to cool cookies completely. (Cookies may be stored at room temperature in an airtight container for up to 1 month.)

5. If using Italian Meringue Buttercream, beat in vanilla extract. To assemble the cupcakes, frost each cupcake generously using an icing spatula or a spoon. Press 1 heart-shaped cookie on top of frosting, allowing a little frosting to poke through the center hole. Sprinkle red glitter over frosting in center hole. Cupcakes are now ready to serve.

Cupcake Tips

These cupcakes are easy to vary: Tint the frosting pink (or any color you like), use different color glitter, or substitute colored sugar or nonpareils.

Irish Coffee Cupcakes

🔵 **HOLIDAY** *St. Patrick's Day*

🔵 **DESCRIPTION** *These cupcakes taste like a real Irish coffee! To create them, I have taken artistic license and placed yellow cupcakes in coffee mugs, sprinkled the cake with Bailey's Irish Cream liqueur, and topped that with whipped cream frosting and chocolate-covered coffee beans. Serve these to adults with a spoon for dessert.*

🔵 **FIELD NOTES** *The instant espresso powder and chocolate-covered espresso beans can be found in specialty food stores and some large supermarkets. I recommend the Medaglia d'Oro brand of espresso powder. Make sure you have mugs or cups that the cupcakes can fit into. They do not have to fit perfectly, but it is best if there is some headroom for the whipped cream to sit inside the cup or mug.*

🔵 **LIFESPAN** *Cupcakes may be baked 2 days ahead; assembled cupcakes are best served the same day. Store refrigerated in airtight container.*

Yield: *12 very adult cupcakes*

INGREDIENTS

1 batch Yellow Cupcakes (page 19), made without paper liners

⅓ cup Bailey's Irish Cream liqueur, or more to taste

2 teaspoons instant espresso powder

Pastry bag

Large star tip

1 batch Whipped Cream Frosting (page 30), prepared through step 1

12 chocolate-covered espresso beans (optional)

DIRECTIONS

1. Place 1 cupcake inside each mug, pressing it down to the bottom.

2. Whisk together liqueur and espresso powder until espresso dissolves. If it doesn't dissolve, heat mixture briefly in a small saucepan over low heat and stir until it does. Pierce each cupcake several times with a bamboo skewer or toothpick. Brush liqueur mixture over each cupcake.

3. Using pastry bag fitted with tip, pipe a large swirl of frosting on top of each cupcake, filling up the remaining space in the mug or cup and/or bringing the whipped cream up above the top of the cup. Top with a chocolate-covered espresso bean, if desired. Cupcakes are now ready to serve. Don't forget the spoon! (You may refrigerate cupcakes for most of the day, but make sure to bring back to room temperature before serving.)

Cupcake Tips

You can make these as boozy as you like by using more (or less) liqueur. You can even add some liqueur to the whipped cream before it is finished whipping.

Shamrock Cupcakes

🍀 **HOLIDAY** *St. Patrick's Day*

🍀 **DESCRIPTION** *Simple yellow cupcakes topped with kelly-green frosting (I use Wilton Icing Color in Kelly Green) and a buttery, crisp shamrock cookie painted with edible gold will bring you the luck of the Irish.*

🍀 **FIELD NOTES** *The cookies can be made way ahead—either the dough or the cookies themselves—so take advantage of the do-ahead steps. Or, since you need very little cookie dough, you could cheat and buy refrigerated sugar cookie dough. You can order the cookie cutter and edible marker from Sweet Celebrations and the edible gold powder from Beryl's (see Resources).*

🍀 **LIFESPAN** *Cupcakes may be baked 2 days ahead; frosted cupcakes are best served the same day. Store at room temperature in airtight container.*

Yield: *24 lucky cupcakes*

INGREDIENTS

Cookies:
1¼ cups all-purpose flour
Pinch of salt
½ cup (1 stick) unsalted butter, at room temperature, cut into tablespoon-size pieces
½ cup sugar
½ teaspoon vanilla extract
1 large egg
1¼-inch shamrock-shaped cookie cutter

Edible gold powder
Vodka
Small, soft artist's brushes
Green edible food marker (optional)

2 batches Yellow Cupcakes (page 19) in paper liners of your choice
1 batch Classic Confectioners' Sugar Frosting (page 26)
Green food coloring

DIRECTIONS

1. To make the cookies, whisk flour and salt together in a small bowl to aerate; set aside. In a large bowl with an electric mixer on medium-high speed, beat butter until creamy, about 2 minutes. Add sugar gradually, beating until light and fluffy, about 3 minutes, scraping down the bowl once or twice. Beat in vanilla extract. Beat in egg, then beat in the flour mixture in 3 additions. Form dough into a flat disc, wrap in plastic wrap, and refrigerate for at least 2 hours, or until firm enough to roll. Dough may be refrigerated overnight. (You may freeze dough for up to 1 month; defrost in refrigerator overnight before proceeding.)

2. Preheat oven to 350°F. Line a jelly-roll pan with parchment paper.

3. Remove dough from refrigerator and roll out to ¼-inch thickness on floured surface; you may need to flour your rolling pin too. Cut out cookies with shamrock-shaped cutter. Transfer cookies to prepared pan, placing them 1 inch apart. (You need only 24 shamrocks, but make as many as you like for snacks!)

4. Bake for about 7 minutes, or until edges have just begun to color; they should stay fairly pale. Slide parchment onto racks to cool cookies completely. (Cookies may be stored at room temperature in an airtight container for up to 1 month.)

5. Place about a teaspoon of gold powder in a small bowl. Add vodka, a couple of drops at a time, stirring with brush until it forms a paint-like consistency. Using the paintbrush, paint the shamrocks gold. Allow to dry. Use green marker to draw leaf veins and details on cookies, if desired.

6. To assemble the cupcakes, tint frosting with green coloring. Frost each cupcake using an icing spatula or a spoon. Insert golden shamrock vertically into frosting. Cupcakes are now ready to serve.

"Real Carrot" Cupcakes

 **HOLIDAY** *Easter*

 **DESCRIPTION** *The classic combo of carrot cake and cream cheese icing is given a twist with cookie crumb "dirt" and candy "carrots" that look as though they are planted in the dirt. Kids of all ages love plucking out the carrot, partially because it is not immediately obvious what it is!*

 **FIELD NOTES** *The key to these are the candy carrots, which can be ordered from Sweet Celebrations (see Resources). These just might be the easiest cupcakes in the book.*

 **LIFESPAN** *Cupcakes may be baked 2 days ahead; frosted cupcakes are best served the same day. Store refrigerated in airtight container.*

Yield: *24 fresh-from-the-garden cupcakes*

 INGREDIENTS

1 batch Carrot Cake Cupcakes (page 24) in green or brown paper liners
1 batch Cream Cheese Frosting (page 29)

1½ cups ground chocolate cookie or graham cracker crumbs (I use Nabisco Famous Chocolate Wafers to make the "dirt" crumbs)
24 sugar candy "carrots"

DIRECTIONS

1. Frost each cupcake generously using an icing spatula or a spoon. Place cookie crumbs in a wide bowl. Hold each cupcake over the bowl. Using a spoon or your fingers, scoop up crumbs and sprinkle a row of cookie crumbs across the cupcake to mimic a row of dirt.

(Excess crumbs will fall back into the bowl and can be reused.)

2. "Plant" a candy carrot as shown in photo, with carrot tops poking above icing and carrot buried below. Cupcakes are now ready to serve.

Easter Basket Cupcakes

🌸 **HOLIDAY** *Easter*

🌸 **DESCRIPTION** *These cupcakes are baked in deeply fluted brown liners (see Resources), which look like little baskets. The liners are necessary as they are stiff enough to hold the basket's "handle" in place. Confectioners' sugar frosting is tinted green and piped out to look like Easter grass, and a piece of licorice forms the handle. For the "eggs," you can use purchased jelly beans or make the tiny marzipan eggs, as described. Wilton Icing Colors in Leaf Green and Sky Blue are perfect for the grass and eggs.*

🌸 **FIELD NOTES** *Marzipan is not the same thing as almond paste. It is sweeter and much smoother, which is what you need. They are often sold side by side; make sure you buy marzipan. The handles are made out of licorice twists, which you can usually find in red and black. Search out the brown chocolate flavor, if you can; otherwise, use black.*

🌸 **LIFESPAN** *Cupcakes may be baked 2 days ahead; frosted cupcakes are best served the same day. Store at room temperature in airtight container.*

Yield: *24 cupcake baskets*

 INGREDIENTS

Marzipan eggs:
 12 ounces marzipan
 Blue food coloring
 Instant coffee

Cupcakes:
 24 fluted brown paper liners
 1 batch batter from Chocolate Cupcakes
 (page 20)

1 batch Classic Confectioners' Sugar
 Frosting (page 26)
Green food coloring
Pastry bag and coupler
Wilton tip #233
24 pieces of chocolate licorice (each about
 6 inches long)

 DIRECTIONS

1. To make the marzipan eggs, knead marzipan until malleable. Knead in a tiny bit of blue coloring for a good robin's egg color. Roll into small balls, about ½ inch across, then elongate slightly to form an egg shape. Pick up bits of instant coffee with fingertips and press onto eggs to create speckles. (Eggs may be made 1 week ahead and stored at room temperature in an airtight container.)

2. To make the cupcakes, preheat oven to 350°F. Place paper liners on two jelly-roll pans (no need for cupcake tins).

3. Divide cupcake batter evenly among liners. Bake for about 17 minutes, or until a toothpick inserted in center shows a few moist crumbs. Cool pans on racks for 5 minutes, then remove cupcakes, still in liners, to cooling racks to cool completely.

4. Tint frosting with green coloring so that it is a nice grassy color. Using pastry bag fitted with tip, pipe grass all over tops of cupcakes.

5. Bend a piece of licorice and insert ends down into frosting and cupcake on two opposite sides of "basket," forming handle. Place a few eggs in center of cupcake. Cupcakes are now ready to serve.

"Spaghetti and Meatballs" Cupcakes

🧁 **HOLIDAY** *April Fool's Day*

🧁 **DESCRIPTION** *These look like chocolate cupcakes topped with a pile of spaghetti, tomato sauce, and meatballs. The spaghetti is made from frosting and the sauce from red gel. The meatballs are a rich chocolate ganache formed into small balls, then rolled in graham cracker crumbs.*

🧁 **FIELD NOTES** *This recipe is all about fakery. No one will really think that spaghetti and meatballs are sitting on your cupcake, but these look real enough to make a great April Fool's treat. You will need six tubes of the red gel (the tubes are tiny!).*

🧁 **LIFESPAN** *Cupcakes may be baked 2 days ahead; frosted cupcakes are best served the same day. Store at room temperature in airtight container.*

Yield: *18 very silly cupcakes*

 INGREDIENTS

Meatballs:
Generous 1 tablespoon heavy cream
2 ounces semisweet chocolate, finely
  chopped
3 tablespoons graham cracker crumbs

1 batch Chocolate Cupcakes (page 20)
  in brown paper liners
1 batch Classic Confectioners' Sugar
  Frosting (page 26)
Pastry bag and coupler
Ateco or Wilton Tip #3
6 tubes Wilton Gel Tube in Red

 DIRECTIONS

1. To make the "meatballs," melt cream and chocolate together in double boiler or microwave; stir until smooth. Cool, then refrigerate overnight.

2. Place graham cracker crumbs in a small bowl. Scoop up little bits of ganache and roll into balls about ¼ inch in diameter (you need 54 "meatballs"). Toss in graham cracker crumbs and roll around to coat thoroughly. "Meatballs" may be refrigerated in an airtight container for up to 1 week.

3. Place cupcakes on clean work surface. Place frosting in pastry bag fitted with tip and pipe strands of "spaghetti" coiled on top of cupcakes, as in photograph. Apply "sauce" by squeezing red gel directly on top of center portion of "spaghetti." Place three "meatballs" on top of sauce. Chill briefly to set. Cupcakes are now ready to serve.

Lemon Meringue Cupcakes

🧁 **HOLIDAY** *Mother's Day*

🧁 **DESCRIPTION** *These cupcakes are sweet and tart. They feature basic yellow cupcakes with a rich, tangy, lemon curd filling, a lemon moistening syrup, and a browned, chewy, sweet meringue topping—just like a lemon meringue pie!*

🧁 **FIELD NOTES** *The best approach is to make the lemon curd up to a week ahead; bake the cupcakes up to 2 days ahead; then fill, moisten, and top them with meringue the day you wish to enjoy them. They are a great Mother's Day dessert that the kids can help make. Kids seem to particularly enjoy squeezing the filling into the center of the cupcakes. Don't be put off by all the steps—you will see that many of the components can be made ahead. You might have some frosting left over. If you want to take the time to do the math, you could prepare a three-quarter batch of frosting by multiplying the ingredients by 0.75. That would give you the perfect amount needed here.*

🧁 **LIFESPAN** *Cupcakes may be baked 2 days ahead; frosted cupcakes are best served the same day. Store at room temperature in airtight container.*

Yield: *24 oh-so-lemony cupcakes*

🔴 INGREDIENTS

Lemon curd:
¼ cup freshly squeezed lemon juice
2 large eggs
1 large egg yolk
¾ cup sugar
6 tablespoons unsalted butter, at room
  temperature, cut into pieces

Lemon syrup:
⅓ cup sugar
⅓ cup water

⅓ cup freshly squeezed lemon juice

Pastry bag and coupler
Ateco or Wilton Tip #12 (or any plain
  round tip with approximately ¼-inch
  opening)
2 batches Yellow Cupcakes (page 19)
  in yellow or white paper liners
1 batch Fluffy Meringue Frosting (page 31)

🔴 DIRECTIONS

1. To make the lemon curd, place lemon juice, eggs, egg yolk, and sugar in a small heavy-bottomed saucepan. Whisk together until thoroughly combined. Place over low-medium heat and whisk occasionally until mixture begins to thicken. Do not let it simmer or boil. Whisk in butter one piece at a time. Continue to cook until mixture is thick enough to mound when dropped by a spoon, about 10 minutes. Remove from heat, let cool to room temperature, and refrigerate in airtight container at least overnight or up to 1 week.

2. To make the lemon syrup, stir sugar and water together in a small saucepan. Bring to a boil over medium-high heat. Swirl pot around to help dissolve sugar. Remove from heat and cool to room temperature. Stir in lemon juice. Lemon syrup is ready to use. Syrup may be refrigerated in airtight container for up to 1 week.

3. Place cupcakes on jellyroll pans. Pierce each several times with a bamboo skewer. Brush lemon syrup over each one, then go over each one again for maximum absorption.

4. Place lemon curd in pastry bag fitted with tip. Insert tip right down into the center of each cupcake. Squeeze to fill with lemon curd. As soon as the top of the cupcake begins to expand and crack, ease up on pressure—the cupcake has taken on as much filling as it can. (Aim for about 1 tablespoon filling per cupcake.) If any lemon curd is oozing out of the top, simply wipe away before frosting. Cupcakes may be made up to this point early in the day of serving.

5. Frost cupcakes with meringue frosting, using a teaspoon to make whirls and swirls on top of the cupcakes—they should look like the tops of little lemon meringue pies. Cupcakes may be made up to this point early in the day of serving.

6. Right before serving, run cupcakes under a hot broiler until meringue just becomes tinged with color. Alternatively, you may use a crème brûlée torch and simply wave it back and forth over the cupcakes to brown the meringue. Cupcakes are now ready to serve.

Breakfast-in-Bed Cupcakes

 **HOLIDAY** *Mother's Day*

 **DESCRIPTION** *I couldn't decide between a classic coffeecake or a jelly doughnut, so this cupcake combines the two with a coffeecake batter, a jelly filling, a streusel top, and a light sprinkling of confectioners' sugar. Use whatever flavor jelly or jam your mom likes.*

 **FIELD NOTES** *These make a very nice Mother's Day surprise, but here is the trick—they are best when freshly made. So get up early, and let your mom sleep in! She deserves it. However, they will still be very good if you make them a day or two ahead and reheat gently in a 250°F oven.*

 **LIFESPAN** *Cupcakes are best served the same day. Store at room temperature in airtight container.*

Yield: *18 what-a-way-to-wake-up cupcakes*

 INGREDIENTS

18 paper liners in your mom's favorite color

1 batch batter and streusel from Crumb Cake Cupcakes (page 22), prepared without fruit or nuts

6 tablespoons jelly or jam of your choice

Confectioners' sugar

 DIRECTIONS

1. Preheat oven to 350°F. Place paper liners in all wells of one 12-cup and one 6-cup cupcake tin.

2. Fill each paper liner about one-quarter of the way full with batter. Place about 1 teaspoon of jelly in the center, then fill with remaining batter. Top with streusel.

3. Bake for about 22 minutes, or until a toothpick inserted into the cake portion of the cupcake shows a few moist crumbs. Cool pans on racks for 5 minutes, then remove cupcakes to cooling racks to cool completely. Dust tops with confectioners' sugar right before serving.

Cupcake Tips

Since these are filled with moist jelly, make sure you are testing with a toothpick in the cake portion of the cupcake and not in the jelly filling. Also, I am a big fan of 100 percent fruit spreads, rather than traditional jams. You get more fruit flavor and less sugar.

Sunflower Cupcakes

HOLIDAY *Mother's Day*

DESCRIPTION *While you can use any cake flavor, I particularly like chocolate for these because the darker color gives a sense of the stem and dirt that you would find with a real sunflower. This cupcake is all about the decoration—each cupcake sports large, gorgeous, sunny-yellow buttercream sunflower petals on top. The center of the flower is made from chocolate sprinkles.*

FIELD NOTES *By placing two shades of yellow buttercream in the same piping bag, you will better approximate the natural variations in actual sunflower petals. I recommend that you use Wilton Icing Color in Lemon Yellow. Depending on where you live, you might know the chocolate sprinkles as "jimmies." Sweet Celebrations has sprinkles made from real chocolate (see Resources), which are much tastier than those available in supermarkets.*

LIFESPAN *Cupcakes may be baked 2 days ahead; frosted cupcakes are best served the same day. Store refrigerated in airtight container.*

Yield: *18 very sunny cupcakes*

INGREDIENTS

1 batch Chocolate Cupcakes (page 20) or other cupcakes of your choice in brown or dark green paper liners
1 batch Italian Meringue Buttercream (page 32)

1½ teaspoons vanilla extract
Yellow food coloring
Pastry bag and coupler
Wilton tip #352
½ cup chocolate sprinkles

DIRECTIONS

1. If the cupcake tops are very peaked, trim to make a level surface.

2. Place buttercream in a large mixing bowl and beat in vanilla extract. Divide the buttercream in half, placing each half in a separate bowl. Add enough food coloring to one half to make a light yellow. Add a greater amount to the other half to make a deeper yellow.

3. Use a small offset spatula to smear a thin coat of either buttercream over the center of each cupcake, covering about a 1-inch circle. This does not have to be perfect (it is for the chocolate sprinkles to stick to later on). Now place the two buttercreams alternately in the same pastry bag fitted with the tip—a couple of tablespoons of each color at a time, which you can assess by eye. This way, when you squeeze the bag, both colors will come out and form subtly shaded petals.

4. To make the sunflowers, visualize a 1-inch circle in the center of each cupcake, which should be easy to do, because it is where you already applied some buttercream. The petals of the sunflower will radiate out from this circle to the edges of the cupcake, leaving that 1-inch center circle open. (Refer to photograph.) Begin at the edge of the circle and, one by one, pipe petals going all the way out to the edge of the cupcake. The petals should be straightish, but a little curve here and there will make them more realistic. Make each new petal right next to the one before. A tiny bit of overlap now and then will also add to the realism. You might need two rows. When you have completed your rings of petals, sprinkle the center with chocolate sprinkles. Cupcakes are now ready to serve.

Cupcake Tips

You can practice piping the petals on a clean plate, then simply scrape up the buttercream and reuse.

Pineapple Upside-Down Cupcakes

🍎 **HOLIDAY** *Memorial Day*

🍎 **DESCRIPTION** *I figured, why not make a cupcake version of pineapple upside-down cakes? They work beautifully. The buttery brown sugar glaze holding in the fruit is as tasty as ever.*

🍎 **FIELD NOTES** *I like these for Memorial Day, or for anytime you need a picnic dessert, because they do not have to be refrigerated and they stay very moist. You will need a plate and fork, but at a picnic you will have those around anyway. Just pack these in disposable plastic containers.*

🍎 **LIFESPAN** *Cupcakes may be baked 1 day ahead. Store at room temperature in airtight container.*

Yield: *18 fruity cupcakes*

 INGREDIENTS

Pineapple topping:
6 tablespoons (¾ stick) unsalted butter,
  at room temperature
1 cup firmly packed light brown sugar
2 cups canned pineapple chunks packed in
  juice, drained

9 maraschino cherries, halved

1 batch batter from Yellow Cupcakes
(page 19)

DIRECTIONS

1. Preheat oven to 350°F. Heavily coat the insides of one 12-cup and one 6-cup cupcake tin with nonstick cooking spray.

2. To make the pineapple topping, melt butter in a saucepan over medium heat. Add brown sugar, stirring occasionally, until sugar bubbles. Divide butter-sugar mixture among cupcake wells.

3. Slice each fan-shaped chunk of pineapple in half so that you end up with thinner fan-shaped chunks. Place 4 of these pieces evenly over the butter-sugar mixture with the broader, rounded part of the fan along the rounded edge of the well. Press half a cherry, rounded side up, into the center.

4. Divide cupcake batter evenly over pineapple topping. Bake for about 17 minutes, or until toothpick inserted in cake part shows a few moist crumbs. Cool pans on racks for about 5 minutes.

5. Run a small icing spatula or thin-bladed knife around cupcakes and invert over a jelly-roll pan. If any of the topping sticks to the tins, simply remove with a spoon and place on top of cupcakes. Cupcakes are now ready to serve.

Mocha Chip Pound Cake Cupcakes

🍮 **HOLIDAY** *Memorial Day*

🍮 **DESCRIPTION** *The basic pound cake batter gets a bunch of miniature semisweet chocolate morsels folded in, along with a bit of instant espresso powder dissolved in Kahlúa liqueur. A dark chocolate ganache glaze partially covers the tops.*

🍮 **FIELD NOTES** *Without the ganache glaze, these pack well for a picnic. They are still portable with the glaze: Just make sure to pack them tightly in a single layer in an airtight container and place them in a cooler to keep them slightly chilled.*

🍮 **LIFESPAN** *Cupcakes may be baked 2 days ahead; glazed cupcakes are best served the same day. Store at room temperature in airtight container.*

Yield: *18 mocha-flavored, chip-filled cupcakes*

 INGREDIENTS

18 paper liners of your choice
1 batch batter from Pound Cake Cupcakes
(page 21; see step 2 below)
2 teaspoons instant espresso powder
2 teaspoons Kahlúa

⅔ cup miniature semisweet chocolate
morsels
1 batch Ganache Glaze and Frosting
(page 28)

 DIRECTIONS

1. Preheat oven to 325°F. Place paper liners in all wells of one 12-cup and one 6-cup cupcake tin.

2. Prepare the cupcake batter as described through the part in step 3 where you have beaten in the vanilla extract. Dissolve the espresso powder in the Kahlúa and beat it into the batter. Proceed with recipe through end of step 3. Fold in chocolate morsels.

3. Divide batter evenly among cupcake wells. Bake for about 25 minutes, or until a toothpick inserted in the center shows a few moist crumbs. Cool pans on racks for 5 minutes, then remove the cupcakes to cooling racks to cool completely.

4. Cool prepared ganache until it has thickened. It should be somewhere between pourable and spreadable—like mayonnaise. Use a teaspoon to pour/spread about a tablespoon on top of each cupcake. You don't have to go to the edges (see photo). Chill briefly to set glaze. Cupcakes are now ready to serve.

Zesty Orange Pound Cake Cupcakes

 **HOLIDAY** *Memorial Day*

 **DESCRIPTION** *Rich buttery pound cake gets a dose of orange zest and a sweet orange glaze.*

 **FIELD NOTES** *Many of us attend picnics or go to friends' homes for Memorial Day, and these pack and travel very well, making a great hostess offering. Make sure the cupcakes are completely cooled before glazing.*

 **LIFESPAN** *Cupcakes may be baked 2 days ahead; glazed cupcakes are best served the same day. Store at room temperature in airtight container.*

Yield: *18 orangey cupcakes*

 INGREDIENTS

18 paper liners of your choice
1 batch batter from Pound Cake Cupcakes (page 21; see step 2 below)
1 tablespoon orange zest

Glaze:
¾ cup confectioners' sugar (or more if necessary)
2 tablespoons freshly squeezed orange juice

 DIRECTIONS

1. Preheat oven to 325°F. Place paper liners in all wells of one 12-cup and one 6-cup cupcake tin.

2. Prepare the cupcake batter as described through the part in step 3 where you have beaten in the vanilla extract. Beat in orange zest. Proceed with recipe. Divide batter evenly among cupcake wells. Bake for about 22 minutes, or until a toothpick inserted in the center shows a few moist crumbs. Cool pans on racks for 5 minutes, then remove the cupcakes to cooling racks to cool completely.

3. To make the glaze, whisk together confectioners' sugar and orange juice until smooth. It should look slightly opaque and be free of any lumps; you might have to whisk vigorously. If you would like to make it thicker you may add more sugar, which will make a more opaque glaze. However, more sugar equals more sweetness, which I do not think is necessary.

4. Use a teaspoon to drizzle glaze on top of cupcakes. Once it is set, you may reglaze to build up the glaze a little bit. Allow the glaze to set and dry. Cupcakes are now ready to serve.

Boston Cream Pie Cupcakes

🧁 **HOLIDAY** *Father's Day*

🧁 **DESCRIPTION** *Just like the famous dessert they are named for, these are comprised of yellow cake, a pastry cream filling, and a dark chocolate glaze. My version of pastry cream is rich with vanilla bean.*

🧁 **FIELD NOTES** *There are a few theories about how Boston cream pie got its name. It is known that the Parker House Hotel in Boston was serving them as early as 1856. Also, during that time, homemakers had pie tins around, but not necessarily cake tins, so cakes might have first been baked in pie tins, yielding a pie-like shape. The Boston cream pie is also the state dessert of Massachusetts. Even if you and your dad don't live anywhere near Boston, this is a great treat to make for him on Father's Day. Note that the glaze can be made a week ahead and the pastry cream filling can be made up to 3 days ahead, so take advantage.*

🧁 **LIFESPAN** *Cupcakes may be baked 2 days ahead; glazed cupcakes are best served the same day. Store at room temperature in airtight container.*

Yield: *24 creamy, chocolatey cupcakes*

INGREDIENTS

Pastry cream:
1⅓ cups milk
1 vanilla bean
4 large egg yolks
⅓ cup sugar
Generous 3 tablespoons all-purpose flour
Pinch of salt

Pastry bag and coupler
Ateco or Wilton Tip #12 (or any plain round tip with approximately ¼-inch opening)
2 batches Yellow Cupcakes (page 19) in brown paper liners
1 batch Ganache Glaze and Frosting (page 28)

DIRECTIONS

1. To make the pastry cream, place milk in a medium-size nonreactive pot. Split vanilla bean down center and scrape all of the tiny seeds into the milk (a tea-spoon or butter knife is great for this). Add the vanilla bean to the milk as well. Bring to a boil over medium heat. Remove from heat, but keep warm. Let bean steep for 15 minutes.

2. Meanwhile, whisk the egg yolks and sugar together in a large bowl until creamy. Whisk in flour and salt until smooth.

3. Remove the vanilla bean from the milk. Reheat milk until it just comes to a simmer. Pour about one-quarter of the warm milk over the egg yolk mix-ture, whisking gently. Add remaining milk and whisk to combine. Immedi-ately pour mixture back into the pot and cook over low-medium heat. Whisk continuously until thickened, about 8 minutes, but do not let it boil. The pastry cream should be thick enough to mound when dropped from a spoon.

4. Allow pastry cream to cool; stir fre-quently to release heat. When almost at room temperature, scrape into airtight container and refrigerate for at least 4 hours or until thoroughly chilled. Pastry cream may be made up to 3 days ahead.

5. To assemble the cupcakes, place pastry cream in pastry bag fitted with tip. Insert tip right down into the center of each cupcake. Squeeze to fill with pas-try cream. As soon as the top of the cupcake begins to expand and crack, ease up on pressure—the cupcake has taken on as much filling as it can. (Aim for about 1 tablespoon filling per cup-cake.) If any pastry cream is oozing out of the top, simply wipe away before glazing.

6. Gently reheat ganache if necessary to bring it to a fluid state. Use a small off-set spatula or a spoon to apply about 1 tablespoon of ganache to the top of each cupcake; cover the top smoothly with ganache. Cupcakes are now ready to serve.

Cupcake Tips

This recipe yields a lot of cupcakes, as it is difficult to make a smaller batch of pastry cream. Why not bring extra cupcakes to uncles, teachers, and friendly neighborhood dads?

Chocolate-for-Breakfast Cupcakes

HOLIDAY *Father's Day*

DESCRIPTION *Chocolate cake batter is combined with the streusel from the master crumb cake recipe—and chopped dried cherries or cranberries and walnuts are thrown in for good measure.*

FIELD NOTES *Why not eat chocolate for breakfast? I draw the line at chocolate chip pancakes—I just cannot bring myself to make them. However, the chocolate cupcake batter is not that sweet on its own, and these cupcakes, with their lack of frosting and just a bit of streusel, make a great breakfast treat.*

LIFESPAN *Cupcakes may be baked 2 days ahead. Store at room temperature in airtight container.*

Yield: 22 *what-a-way-to-wake-up cupcakes*

 INGREDIENTS

22 paper liners of your choice
⅔ cup dried cherries or cranberries, chopped
⅔ cup walnut halves, toasted (see page 13) and finely chopped

1 batch batter from Chocolate Cupcakes (page 20)
1 batch streusel from Crumb Cake Cupcakes (page 22)

 DIRECTIONS

1. Preheat oven to 350°F. Place paper liners in 22 wells of two 12-cup cupcake tins.

2. Fold the chopped cherries and walnuts into the cupcake batter. Fill each paper liner about one-quarter of the way full with batter. Top with a bit of streusel, then fill wells with remaining batter.

Top with remaining streusel. Bake for about 25 minutes, or until a toothpick inserted in center shows a few moist crumbs. Cool pans on racks for 5 minutes, then remove cupcakes to cooling racks to cool completely. Cupcakes are now ready to serve.

Bananas Foster Cupcakes

🔶 **HOLIDAY** *Father's Day*

🔶 **DESCRIPTION** *Yellow cupcakes get some sweet ripe bananas folded into the batter. Then more bananas are sautéed with butter, caramelized with brown sugar, and flambéed with rum! Whipped cream crowns it all. You will want to serve these in individual bowls.*

🔶 **FIELD NOTES** *Bananas Foster is a classic dessert hailing from New Orleans, usually served with vanilla ice cream. Here it is given the cupcake treatment and dished up with whipped cream instead.*

🔶 **LIFESPAN** *Cupcakes may be baked 2 days ahead. Store at room temperature in airtight container. Assembled cupcakes are best served immediately.*

Yield: *12 New Orleans–style cupcakes*

INGREDIENTS

1 batch batter from Yellow Cupcakes
(page 19; see step 2 below)
¼ teaspoon ground cinnamon
¼ teaspoon ground nutmeg
8 ripe bananas
¼ cup (½ stick) unsalted butter, cut into
tablespoon-size pieces

¾ cup firmly packed light brown sugar
¼ cup rum, light, gold, or dark
2 batches Whipped Cream Frosting,
prepared through step 1 (page 30; may
be made all at once)

DIRECTIONS

1. Preheat oven to 350°F. Coat the insides of one 12-cup cupcake tin with non-stick cooking spray.

2. Prepare cupcake batter through step 2. Whisk cinnamon and nutmeg into the flour mixture. Proceed through step 3. Cut 2 of the bananas into ¼-inch slices and fold into batter. Divide batter evenly among cupcake wells. Bake for about 18 minutes, or until a toothpick inserted in the center shows a few moist crumbs. Cool pan on rack for 5 minutes, then remove cupcakes to a cooling rack to cool completely.

3. Slice remaining 6 bananas crosswise through the middle, then cut each piece lengthwise, so each banana is cut into quarters. Heat 2 tablespoons butter in a large sauté pan. Place half of the banana quarters in the butter and cook over medium-high heat for about 4 minutes, or until browned on the bottom. Flip over each banana slice, sprin-

kle with half the brown sugar, and continue to cook until the bottoms are browned and the sugar is caramelized.

4. Add half of the rum to the pan, and allow it to heat. Carefully ignite to flambé the bananas. There are a couple of ways to do this. If you have a gas stove, you can carefully tilt the pan, and if a flame licks over the side, it will ignite the rum. Alternatively, you can remove the pan from direct heat and ignite the contents with a match placed along the edge of the pan. Transfer bananas and all the juices to a warm bowl. Repeat with remaining butter, bananas, brown sugar, and rum.

5. Split cupcakes vertically. Place cupcake halves side by side in individual bowls. Spoon flambéed bananas, any juices, and whipped cream right down in between the cake halves. Cupcakes are now ready to serve.

Ice Cream Cone Cupcakes

🌸 **HOLIDAY** *Fourth of July*

🌸 **DESCRIPTION** *At first glance, these look like real ice cream cones, complete with a soft serve–like swirl of "ice cream" on top and covered with sprinkles (or jimmies, depending on where you live). The cupcake batter is baked in ice cream cones for a very realistic look. The "ice cream" is actually frosting! Needless to say, kids go nuts over these. Warning: They are very sweet.*

🌸 **FIELD NOTES** *I associate summers with the ice cream man, who used to come to the beach in his truck every afternoon. Around two o'clock we would hear the bells ringing, and we would all go running after the truck, digging out the money that was stashed in our shoes. So I think these cupcakes are a perfect accompaniment to midsummer holiday parties.*

🌸 **LIFESPAN** *Cupcakes may be baked 1 day ahead; frosted cones are best served the same day. Store at room temperature in airtight container.*

Yield: *24 melt-in-your-mouth cupcakes*

INGREDIENTS

24 flat-bottomed wafer cones
1 batch batter from Chocolate Cupcakes
(page 20)
2 batches Fluffy Meringue Frosting
(page 31; may be made all at once)

Pastry bag
Large star tip
2½ cups multicolored or chocolate
sprinkles

DIRECTIONS

1. Preheat oven to 350°F. Place cones in all wells of two 12-cup cupcake tins, wadding up aluminum foil around base of cones to steady them.

2. Divide chocolate cupcake batter evenly among cones. The batter should come to within ½ inch of the top edge of cone.

3. Bake for about 30 minutes, or until a toothpick inserted in center shows a few moist crumbs. Cool pans completely on racks.

4. Place frosting in pastry bag fitted with tip, and make a large, multilayered swirl on top of each cone. You want it to look like a soft-serve ice cream cone. Allow to sit for 5 minutes for frosting to set a bit. Place sprinkles in a small bowl. One at a time, carefully and gently roll the frosting around in the sprinkles until completely and evenly covered.

5. Place cones back in cupcake tins, with fresh aluminum foil wedged around bottoms to store safely so they don't tip over. Cupcakes are now ready to serve!

Cupcake Tips

You can pick the sprinkles up and scatter them over the frosting instead of rolling the frosting in the sprinkles, but you will not get as good coverage. Either way, you will probably have sprinkles left over, but it is easier to start with more, rather than less.

By-the-Beach Cupcakes

🔹 **HOLIDAY** *Fourth of July*

🔹 **DESCRIPTION** *Yellow cupcakes are turned into a mini beach! Tint the frosting blue for water, then add a graham-cracker-crumb sandy beach and a paper umbrella! I like to use Wilton Icing Color in Sky Blue.*

🔹 **FIELD NOTES** *These are very easy to make. Even if you spend Independence Day in your own backyard, these will put you in a summery holiday mood. The paper umbrellas can be found at party supply stores.*

🔹 **LIFESPAN** *Cupcakes may be baked 2 days ahead; frosted cupcakes are best served the same day. Store at room temperature in airtight container.*

Yield: *12 beachy-keen cupcakes*

 INGREDIENTS

½ batch Classic Confectioners' Sugar
  Frosting (page 26)
Blue food coloring

1 batch Yellow Cupcakes (page 19)
  in paper liners of your choice
1¼ cups graham cracker crumbs
12 colorful paper umbrellas

DIRECTIONS

1. Tint the frosting a pretty blue water color. Frost cupcakes using an icing spatula or a spoon.

2. Place graham cracker crumbs in a wide bowl. Hold each cupcake over bowl. Using a spoon or your fingers, sprinkle graham cracker crumbs generously over half of the frosting to make your "beach." (Excess crumbs will fall back into the bowl and can be reused.) Make sure remaining exposed "water" looks like waves by making little peaks of frosting with the back of a spoon. Insert umbrella into the graham cracker crumbs. Cupcakes are now ready to serve.

Cupcake Tips

Piping gel is a flavorless, tasteless, clear gel that can be added to blue-tinted frosting to make it look a bit more like water. It helps give it a little more translucency and shine. You can find it where cake-decorating ingredients are sold. Also, if you want to make the cupcakes a little fancier, look for tiny sugar shells or starfish from cake-decorating supply stores and place one on each "beach."

Strawberry Shortcake Cupcakes

HOLIDAY *Fourth of July*

DESCRIPTION *Yellow cupcakes are layered with sweetened strawberries and whipped cream for a summery holiday treat.*

FIELD NOTES *These must be served in a bowl to catch all the luscious berry juices. Shortcakes are typically made with biscuits, often baking powder biscuits. Some folks like the dessert made with cake instead, and this version fits that bill. This will please the kids in the family too, of course.*

LIFESPAN *Cupcakes may be baked 2 days ahead; store in airtight container. Assembled cupcakes must be served immediately.*

Yield: *12 "shortcake" cupcakes*

 INGREDIENTS

1 batch batter from Yellow Cupcakes
(page 19)
6 cups sliced strawberries
¾ cup sugar

2 batches Whipped Cream Frosting,
prepared through step 1 (page 30; may
be made all at once)

DIRECTIONS

1. Preheat oven to 350°F. Coat the insides
of one 12-cup cupcake tin with nonstick cooking spray.

2. Divide batter evenly among cupcake
wells. Bake for about 18 minutes, or
until a toothpick inserted in the center
shows a few moist crumbs. Cool pan
on rack for 5 minutes, then remove
cupcakes to a cooling rack to cool
completely.

3. Place half of the strawberries in a mixing bowl with the sugar and lightly

crush and blend using a potato masher.
Stir in remaining berries and allow to
sit for 15 minutes.

4. Split cupcakes in half horizontally.
Place bottoms of cupcakes, cut side up,
in individual bowls. Top with some
berries and juices and whipped cream
frosting. Crown with tops of cupcakes,
rounded side up, then top with remaining berries, juices, and frosting.
Cupcakes are now ready to serve.

I Live for Chocolate Cupcakes

🍫 **HOLIDAY** *National Chocolate Cupcake Day (October 18)*

🍫 **DESCRIPTION** *These cupcakes feature chocolate cake, a chocolate mousse filling, chocolate buttercream, and loads of chocolate curls on top. The optional hint of real gold on top is extra special—and edible! Eat these on a plate with a fork in small bites accompanied by a strong cup of coffee or a cold glass of milk.*

🍫 **FIELD NOTES** *What is better than dark chocolate? More dark chocolate! It is my favorite kind, and the more bittersweet, the better. My friend Marcel Desaulniers came up with the "death-by-chocolate" concept for his books, so I would not want to step on his toes by borrowing his description. While musing about this one day it occurred to me that folks often say "I live for chocolate," so that is how these got their name. Serve these at a dinner party and I guarantee your guests' eyes will light up and smiles will erupt all around. The gold leaf can be found at art supply stores and some cake-decorating supply stores. Just make sure it is at least 22 karat for it to be safe to eat.*

🍫 **LIFESPAN** *Cupcakes may be baked 2 days ahead; frosted cupcakes are best served the same day. Store refrigerated in airtight container.*

Yield: *18 decadent, over-the-top cupcakes*

INGREDIENTS

Chocolate mousse:
½ cup heavy cream
3 ounces bittersweet chocolate, melted
and cooled

Pastry bag and coupler
Ateco or Wilton Tip #12 (or any plain
round tip with approximately ¼-inch
opening)

1 batch Chocolate Cupcakes (page 20)
in gold foil liners
Block of bittersweet chocolate
1½ batches Italian Meringue Buttercream
(page 32; may be made all at once)
11 ounces bittersweet chocolate, melted
and slightly cooled
Large star tip
Gold leaf (optional)

DIRECTIONS

1. To make the chocolate mousse, in a medium-size chilled bowl using an electric mixer, beat cream until soft peaks form. Fold in melted chocolate until mixture is smooth. Refrigerate until chilled.

2. Place mousse in pastry bag fitted with #12 tip and insert tip right down into the center of each cupcake. Squeeze to fill with mousse. As soon as the top of the cupcake begins to expand and crack, ease up on pressure—the cupcake has taken on as much filling as it can. (Aim for about 1 tablespoon filling per cupcake.) If any mousse is oozing out of the top, simply wipe away before frosting. Refrigerate cupcakes while you proceed.

3. To make chocolate curls, warm up the block of chocolate in your hands. Use a vegetable peeler to shave off shavings and curls. You need about ⅓ cup of shavings/curls. (It is easier to shave a larger piece of chocolate, but a 1-ounce block will give you the amount you need).

4. Place the buttercream in a large mixing bowl and beat in the cooled melted chocolate. Using pastry bag fitted with large star tip, frost each cupcake with a large swirl on top. Sprinkle chocolate shavings on top of cupcakes. Use tweezers to pick up a small piece of gold leaf and place on top, if desired. Cupcakes are now ready to serve.

Cupcake Tips

To bring these into a very adult realm, sprinkle Kahlúa, Grand Marnier, or rum on the cupcakes before filling them with mousse.

Chocolate, Chocolate, Chocolate Cupcakes

🔸 **HOLIDAY** *National Chocolate Cupcake Day (October 18)*

- -

🔸 **DESCRIPTION** *These cupcakes feature chocolate cake with white chocolate bits folded into the batter and milk chocolate buttercream on top. Crowning the top are curls and shavings of white, milk, and semisweet chocolate.*

- -

🔸 **FIELD NOTES** *The name of the recipe refers to the fact that there are three kinds of chocolate in this cupcake—white, milk, and semisweet. For these cupcakes I like to use the fancy, deeply fluted brown paper liners available from Beryl's (see Resources). To make the white chocolate bits for folding into the batter, simply chop up a block of white chocolate. I find these pieces to be more sophisticated than typical morsels.*

- -

🔸 **LIFESPAN** *Cupcakes may be baked 2 days ahead; frosted cupcakes are best served the same day. Store refrigerated in airtight container.*

Yield: *24 seriously chocolatey cupcakes*

 INGREDIENTS

24 fluted brown paper liners
¾ cup chopped white chocolate (pieces should be about ¼ inch in size)
1 batch batter from Chocolate Cupcakes (page 20)
1½ batches Italian Meringue Buttercream (page 32; may be made all at once)

11 ounces milk chocolate, melted and slightly cooled
Pastry bag
Large star tip
1 block each of white, milk, and semisweet chocolate (see Cupcake Tips)

DIRECTIONS

1. Preheat oven to 350°F. Place paper liners on two jelly-roll pans (no need for cupcake tins).

2. Fold chopped white chocolate into cupcake batter. Divide among cupcake liners. Bake for about 17 minutes, or until a toothpick inserted in center shows a few moist crumbs. Cool pans on racks for 5 minutes, then remove cupcakes, still in liners, to cooling racks to cool completely.

3. Place the buttercream in a large mixing bowl and beat in cooled melted milk chocolate. Using pastry bag fitted with large star tip, frost each cupcake with a large swirl on top.

4. To make the chocolate curls, warm up a block of chocolate in your hands. Use a vegetable peeler to shave off shavings and curls. Do this with all three chocolates. Toss them together in a small bowl for a total of about ½ cup of shavings/curls. Sprinkle shavings on top of cupcakes. Cupcakes are now ready to serve.

Cupcake Tips

You need only about 2 ounces total of the three chocolates for the shavings, but it is easier to make your shavings from larger blocks of chocolate.

Ghostly Cupcakes

🔶 **HOLIDAY** *Halloween*

🔶 **DESCRIPTION** *These cupcakes look like little ghosts. Faces can be painted on their fondant draping to make them look friendly or spooky.*
Underneath is chocolate cake and vanilla frosting. If you use the Classic Confectioners' Sugar Frosting, these will be quite sweet.

🔶 **FIELD NOTES** *Needless to say, kids go crazy over these ghosts. Even if they look scary, little kids love 'em because they can eat 'em! You will need standard-size cupcake tins as well as miniature-size ones. You do not need paper liners for this recipe. The rolled fondant, which is very different from our recipe for Poured Fondant Glaze, can be purchased from any cake-decorating supply store or through mail-order, as can the edible marker.*

🔶 **LIFESPAN** *Cupcakes may be baked 2 days ahead; frosted cupcakes are best served the same day. Store at room temperature in airtight container if using Classic Confectioners' Sugar Frosting; refrigerate in airtight container if using Italian Meringue Buttercream.*

Yield: *14 haunting cupcakes plus 2 extra mini cupcakes to munch*

INGREDIENTS

1 batch batter from Chocolate Cupcakes
(page 20)
1 batch Classic Confectioners' Sugar
Frosting (page 26) or Italian Meringue
Buttercream (page 32)

Confectioners' sugar
28 ounces white rolled fondant, such as
    Wilton Pure White Rolled Fondant
Black edible food marker

DIRECTIONS

1. Preheat oven to 350°F. Have available one 12-cup cupcake tin, one 6-cup cupcake tin, and two 12-cup miniature cupcake tins. You will be using 14 of the standard-size wells and 16 of the miniature ones (the two extra are from extra batter). Coat the insides of these with nonstick cooking spray.

2. Fill the prepared cupcake wells with batter. Bake for about 22 minutes, or until a toothpick inserted in the center shows a few moist crumbs. The mini ones will bake in less time, so keep an eye on them and begin checking them at 15 minutes. Cool pans on racks for 5 minutes, then remove cupcakes to cooling racks to cool completely.

3. To assemble your ghosts, trim tops of standard-size cupcakes if necessary to make a flat surface. Place a large cupcake upside down. Place a dab of frosting on top to act as glue for a mini cupcake, which should be placed on top, rounded side up. Use a small icing spatula to spread frosting all over the stacked cupcakes, covering tops and all sides.

4. Sprinkle work surface with confectioners' sugar. Roll out a 2-ounce piece of fondant to a 7-inch circle. Use a large icing spatula to help loosen it from work surface. Lift carefully with fingers and center and drape it over frosted cupcakes. Use clean, dry hands to smooth fondant so that it drapes down the sides and looks like a little ghost. Trim bottom so that it is flush with work surface. Use a large offset icing spatula slid underneath the ghost to transfer it to serving platter. Use edible marker to make eyes or other facial features. Cupcakes are now ready to serve.

Cupcake Tips

It is sometimes helpful to have a long bamboo skewer handy to insert through the two stacked cupcakes. You can use it as a handle as you frost them. Remember that the frosting does not have to look perfect—it will be covered by fondant.

Hairy Spider Cupcakes

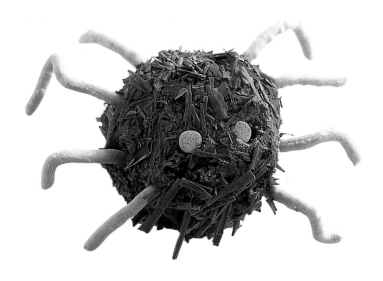

🕷 **HOLIDAY** *Halloween*

🕷 **DESCRIPTION** *These cupcakes are delightfully creepy. The "hair" is chocolate shavings, and to keep them dark and sinister looking, they are chocolate through and through—chocolate cake and frosting, in addition to the "hair." The legs are made from chow mein noodles. I use small round confetti candies for eyes, but you could use anything small and round, such as a bit of contrasting colored frosting or another candy/décor.*

🕷 **FIELD NOTES** *These are messy to make—get the kids involved! Even though the cupcakes themselves are not round, they end up being very round after they are rolled in the frosting and shaved chocolate. Make sure the frosting is very soft. You need three 12-cup miniature-size cupcake tins for this recipe. This is the one recipe in the book where I ask you to halve a cake recipe. You can, of course, make the whole recipe, but you will have more than 70 spiders and have to bake many batches, as I assume you do not have enough cupcake tins to make 70 mini cupcakes!*

🕷 **LIFESPAN** *Cupcakes may be baked 2 days ahead; frosted cupcakes are best served the same day. Store at room temperature in airtight container.*

Yield: *36 creepy, crawly cupcakes*

INGREDIENTS

½ batch batter from Chocolate Cupcakes (page 20)

12-ounce block of semisweet chocolate

2 batches Fudge Frosting (page 27; may be made all at once)

3 cups chow mein noodles

72 small edible confetti decorations

DIRECTIONS

1. Preheat oven to 350°F. Coat the insides of three 12-cup miniature cupcake tins with nonstick cooking spray.

2. Divide batter among cupcake wells and bake for approximately 15 minutes, or until a toothpick inserted in center shows a few moist crumbs. Cool pans on racks for 5 minutes, then remove the cupcakes to cooling racks to cool completely.

3. Use a sharp chef's knife to shave chocolate shavings off of the block of semisweet chocolate. Simply run the knife down one of the edges of the chocolate block and you should get shards and shavings; set aside in a medium bowl. Line a jelly-roll pan with parchment paper or foil; set aside.

4. Make sure frosting is very soft. Place about 1 cup of frosting in a small bowl. Pick up a cupcake and literally roll it around in the frosting. This is not an exact science—and it is very messy! You are just trying to get a coating of frosting all over the cupcake for the chocolate shavings to stick to. Use your fingertips to push the cupcake around on the surface of the frosting. It is fine if it is thicker in some areas. Remove cupcake from bowl and immediately roll the cupcake around in the chocolate shavings. This is when the cupcake takes on a round shape. Keep rolling it around until it is completely covered. Transfer to prepared jelly-roll pan.

5. Repeat with all the cupcakes. Insert 8 chow mein "legs" into each spider and also give each one 2 eyes, as in photograph. Chill until frosting firms up; bring back to room temperature before serving. Cupcakes are now ready to serve.

Tombstone Cupcakes

🧁 **HOLIDAY** *Halloween*

🧁 **DESCRIPTION** *Chocolate cake and frosting get a covering of chocolate cookie crumb "dirt." A chocolate-covered graham cracker is the perfect shape for a tombstone.*

🧁 **FIELD NOTES** *There are several chocolate-covered graham crackers on the market. Keebler Fudge Shoppe Deluxe Grahams have a good "tombstone" shape. While you could just make additional frosting and use a small round tip to write the "RIPs," it is much easier to use the Wilton Icing Writer, which is a very convenient and easy-to-use tool for writing on small areas (see Resources).*

🧁 **LIFESPAN** *Cupcakes may be baked 2 days ahead; frosted cupcakes are best served the same day. Store at room temperature in airtight container.*

Yield: *18 cemetery-friendly cupcakes*

 INGREDIENTS

1 batch Chocolate Cupcakes (page 20) in brown paper liners
1½ batches Fudge Frosting (page 27; may be made all at once)

1¾ cups ground chocolate cookie crumbs (I use Nabisco Famous Chocolate Wafers)
18 chocolate-covered graham crackers
Wilton Icing Writer in color of your choice

 DIRECTIONS

1. Frost each cupcake generously using an icing spatula or a spoon. Place chocolate cookie crumbs in a wide bowl. Hold each cupcake over the bowl. Using a spoon or your fingers, scoop up crumbs and sprinkle over the frosting to cover completely. You want the surface to look like dirt. (Excess crumbs will fall back into the bowl and can be reused.)

2. Place chocolate-covered graham crackers flat on work surface. Use Icing Writer to write "RIP" on each one. (If you can fit it, you might also want to add a person's name, as a joke, but they'll have to have a very short name!) Press graham cracker "tombstone" into "dirt" (see photo for placement). Cupcakes are now ready to serve.

Mummy Cupcakes

🧁 **HOLIDAY** *Halloween*

🧁 **DESCRIPTION** *The base for these cupcakes is a chewy chocolate brownie. The look is that of a mummy with friendly but spooky eyes peering out from beneath his wraps!*

🧁 **FIELD NOTES** *Getting the mummies' wraps to look right might take some practice, so try it a few times on a clean plate, then scrape up the frosting and reuse. Ateco tip #47 has one side that will make smooth ribbons and one side that makes ridges. Use the smooth side.*

🧁 **LIFESPAN** *Cupcakes may be baked 2 days ahead; frosted cupcakes are best served the same day. Store at room temperature in airtight container if using Classic Confectioners' Sugar Frosting; refrigerate in airtight container if using Italian Meringue Buttercream.*

Yield: *18 mummified cupcakes*

INGREDIENTS

1 batch Brownie Cupcakes (page 25) in white paper liners

1 batch Classic Confectioners' Sugar Frosting (page 26) or Italian Meringue Buttercream (page 32)

1½ teaspoons vanilla extract (if using Italian Meringue Buttercream)

Pastry bag and coupler

Ateco tip #47

Yellow paste or gel food coloring

Ateco or Wilton tip #12

36 semisweet chocolate morsels

DIRECTIONS

1. Place cupcakes on clean work surface. Place frosting in a large mixing bowl. If using Italian Meringue Buttercream, beat in vanilla extract. Place in pastry bag and, using smooth side of tip #47, form mummy's wraps on top of cupcakes, leaving some brownie showing through for eyes. Think about what it looks like to make a head wrap around an injured person! There should be angled wraps on the top of the mummy's head, with some angled and some horizontal ones beneath its eyes. Each wrap should overlap the previous one to give a realistic look. This is one cupcake where the photo example really is worth a thousand words!

2. Tint remaining frosting a nice yellow for glowing eyes! Use pastry bag fitted with tip #12 to pipe rounds for eyes. Insert chocolate morsels, tip side down, in center of eyes to make irises. Make sure you can see some yellow around the morsel. Cupcakes are now ready to serve.

Pumpkin Cupcakes

🎃 **HOLIDAY** *Halloween*

🎃 **DESCRIPTION** *Here moist carrot cake is topped with orange-tinted Italian Meringue Buttercream piped to look like a pumpkin with a green stem.*

🎃 **FIELD NOTES** *Many of the Halloween cupcakes in this book are for the kids. This one is a little more grown up, for the adults at the party. Use the smooth side of Ateco tip #47 to form the pumpkin. When making the cap and stem, both sides of the tip will be used.*

🎃 **LIFESPAN** *Cupcakes may be baked 2 days ahead; frosted cupcakes are best served the same day. Store refrigerated in airtight container.*

Yield: *24 jack o' lantern cupcakes*

INGREDIENTS

1 batch Carrot Cake Cupcakes (page 24)
in green or brown paper liners
1½ batches Italian Meringue Buttercream
(page 32; may be made all at once)
2 teaspoons vanilla extract

Green paste or gel food coloring, such as
Wilton Icing Color in Moss Green
Orange paste or gel food coloring, such as
Wilton Icing Color in Orange
Pastry bag and coupler
Ateco tip #47

DIRECTIONS

1. Place cupcakes on clean work surface. Place the buttercream in a large mixing bowl and beat in vanilla extract. Place about 1½ cups buttercream in a small bowl; tint it green. Tint the remaining portion orange.

2. Using pastry bag and smooth side of tip #47, pipe curved vertical ribbons of orange buttercream on top of cupcake to make a pumpkin shape. As you pipe the ribbons that are to either the left or the right of center, gently curve them in the appropriate direction to give a sense of three-dimensional roundness— like a real pumpkin. The cupcake should be completely covered with ribbons of buttercream.

3. Again using tip #47, pipe a green buttercream stem and stem cap going up and down in an upside-down fan shape at the top center of the cupcake, using both the smooth and ridged side of the tip. This will give a sense of texture (see photo). Cupcakes are now ready to serve.

Spider Web Cupcakes

🔷 **HOLIDAY** *Halloween*

🔷 **DESCRIPTION** *Chocolate cupcakes are topped with chocolate ganache glaze, and white chocolate "spider webs" are formed on top.*

🔷 **FIELD NOTES** *The key to making successful "webs" is to have the ganache glaze and the melted white chocolate both in a fluid state, so that when you draw your knife through them, they pull into attractive shapes (this will make sense when you get to that point in the recipe).*

🔷 **LIFESPAN** *Cupcakes may be baked 2 days ahead; glazed cupcakes are best served the same day. Store at room temperature in airtight container.*

Yield: *18 chocolate web cupcakes*

INGREDIENTS

1½ batches Ganache Glaze and Frosting
(page 28; may be made all at once)

1 batch Chocolate Cupcakes (page 20)
in brown paper liners
6 ounces white chocolate, finely chopped

DIRECTIONS

1. Make sure ganache is in a fluid state. Use a small offset spatula to apply ganache generously and smoothly to the top of each cupcake.

2. Melt the white chocolate in a double boiler or in a small bowl in the microwave and place in a zipper-top plastic bag (you will have to use a few bags). Cut a small opening in the bottom corner of the bag.

3. Place the corner of the bag over the center of a cupcake. Squeeze gently and pipe a spiral all the way to the outer edge of the cupcake (about 4 loops around the cupcake). Immediately, while the glaze and chocolate are still soft, again starting at the center, draw the tip of a thin, sharp knife out toward the edge of the cupcake in a straight line. Repeat this in a spoke pattern going around the cupcake (about 6 spokes)—voilà, webs!

4. Repeat step 3 for remaining cupcakes. Chill cupcakes briefly until glaze is set. Cupcakes are now ready to serve.

Cupcake Tips

If you like, search out tiny candy spider decorations from cake-decorating supply stores and place one on each "web."

Pumpkin-Filled Spice Cupcakes

HOLIDAY *Thanksgiving*

DESCRIPTION *These start simply enough with a basic yellow cake batter, but for this recipe I have added some pumpkin pie spices to the batter. A cheesecake-like pumpkin filling makes for a creamy surprise. They are simply frosted and topped with a sprinkling of nuts.*

FIELD NOTES *These are perfect for a Thanksgiving party where there will be lots of kids. Instead of having to wait for a slice of pie, they can grab a cupcake and be off playing with their cousins and friends in no time.*

LIFESPAN *Cupcakes may be baked 2 days ahead; frosted cupcakes are best served the same day. Store at room temperature in airtight container.*

Yield: *12 creamy filled cupcakes*

 INGREDIENTS

12 paper liners of your choice
1 batch batter from Yellow Cupcakes
(page 19; see step 2 below)
1 teaspoon ground cinnamon
1 teaspoon ground ginger
¼ teaspoon ground nutmeg
⅛ teaspoon ground cloves

Pumpkin filling:
3 tablespoons plus 2 teaspoons unsalted
butter, at room temperature
7½ ounces cream cheese, at room
temperature

Scant 1 teaspoon vanilla extract
1⅓ cups confectioners' sugar, whisked
before measuring
3 tablespoons canned pumpkin puree

Pastry bag and coupler
Ateco or Wilton Tip #12 (or any plain
round tip with approximately ¼-inch
opening)
½ batch Classic Confectioners' Sugar
Frosting (page 26)
¾ cup pecan halves, toasted (see page 13)
and chopped

DIRECTIONS

1. Preheat oven to 350°F. Place paper liners in all wells of one 12-cup cupcake tin.

2. Prepare cupcake batter as described through step 2, then whisk in the spices listed above. Proceed with recipe as directed.

3. To make the pumpkin filling, in a large bowl with an electric mixer on medium-high speed, beat butter, cream cheese, and vanilla extract until creamy, about 3 minutes. Add confectioners' sugar gradually, beating until light and fluffy, about 3 minutes, scraping down the bowl once or twice. Beat in pumpkin puree.

4. Place filling in pastry bag fitted with tip. Insert tip right down into the center of each cupcake. Squeeze to fill with filling. As soon as the top of the cupcake begins to expand and crack, ease up on pressure—the cupcake has taken on as much filling as it can. (Aim for about 1 tablespoon filling per cupcake.) If any filling is oozing out of the top, simply wipe away before frosting.

5. Frost each cupcake with the frosting using an icing spatula or a spoon. Sprinkle with pecans. Cupcakes are now ready to serve.

Caramel Apple Cupcakes

HOLIDAY *Thanksgiving*

DESCRIPTION *Sour cream cupcake batter is filled with chunks of tart apples and walnuts and then topped with streusel and caramel.*

FIELD NOTES *Instead of an apple pie at Thanksgiving, make these apple-and-walnut-filled cupcakes as a twist on a traditional dessert offering.*
Because the streusel and caramel are sweet, it's best to use tart apples, such as Granny Smith, to balance out the flavors.

LIFESPAN *Cupcakes are best served the same day. Store at room temperature in airtight container.*

Yield: *18 sticky caramel cupcakes*

 INGREDIENTS

18 paper liners of your choice
⅔ cup peeled and diced Granny Smith apples
⅔ cup walnut halves, toasted (see page 13) and chopped

1 batch batter and streusel from Crumb Cake Cupcakes (page 22), prepared without fruit or nuts
18 Kraft caramels

 DIRECTIONS

1. Preheat oven to 350°F. Place paper liners in all wells of one 12-cup and one 6-cup cupcake tin.

2. Fold the chopped apples and walnuts into the plain cupcake batter. Fill each paper liner about one-quarter of the way full with batter. Top with a bit of streusel, then fill with remaining batter. Top with remaining streusel. Bake for about 22 minutes, or until a toothpick inserted in the center shows a few moist crumbs. Cool pans on racks for 5 minutes, then remove cupcakes to cooling racks to cool completely.

3. Melt caramels in top of double boiler or in microwave. Drizzle caramel over tops of cooled cupcakes using a fork or teaspoon. Cupcakes are now ready to serve.

Snowball Cupcakes

🟠 **HOLIDAY** *Christmas*

🟠 **DESCRIPTION** *You can use any cake flavor for this recipe, but I suggest the white or yellow cake batters. These cupcakes feature cake, icing, and fluffy white coconut— they look like snowballs. If you use the Classic Confectioners' Sugar Frosting, they will be sweeter.*

🟠 **FIELD NOTES** *It might seem odd, but once covered in frosting and coconut, these really do look round! The process is messy, but kids can help. Make sure to have the frosting very soft, or the technique of applying it won't work. The reason you work with a little bit of frosting at a time is so that if any crumbs fall into it, they are easy to pick out and will not get on subsequent "snowballs."*

🟠 **LIFESPAN** *Cupcakes may be baked 2 days ahead; frosted cupcakes are best served the same day. Store at room temperature in airtight container if using Classic Confectioners' Sugar Frosting; refrigerate in airtight container if using Italian Meringue Buttercream.*

Yield: *12 wintry cupcakes*

 INGREDIENTS

6 cups sweetened flaked coconut

2 batches Classic Confectioners' Sugar Frosting (page 26) or Italian Meringue Buttercream (page 32; may be made all at once)

1 batch White Cupcakes (page 18) or Yellow Cupcakes (page 19), baked without paper liners

 DIRECTIONS

1. Place coconut in a medium-size bowl; set aside. Line a jelly-roll pan with parchment paper or aluminum foil; set aside.

2. Make sure frosting is very soft. Place about 2 cups of frosting in a small bowl. Pick up a cupcake and literally roll it around in the frosting. This is not an exact science, and it is very messy! You are just trying to get a coating of frosting all over the cupcake for the coconut to stick to. Use your fingertips to push the cupcake around on the surface of the frosting. It is fine if the frosting is thicker in some areas.

3. Remove cupcake from bowl of frosting and immediately roll it around in the coconut. This is when the cupcake takes on a round shape. Keep rolling it around until it is completely covered. Transfer to prepared jelly-roll pan.

4. Repeat with all the cupcakes. Chill until buttercream firms up; bring back to room temperature before serving. Cupcakes are now ready to serve.

Cupcake Tips

My absolute favorite way to serve these is in a wide, shallow soup bowl, with a scoop of vanilla ice cream alongside and melted chocolate Ganache Glaze (page 28) pooled in the bottom—*yum!*

Peppermint Twist Cupcakes

🍥 **HOLIDAY** *Christmas*

🍥 **DESCRIPTION** *These cupcakes feature chocolate cake studded with bits of minty candy cane. Crowning the top is a swirl of white chocolate buttercream with more crushed candy cane sprinkled on top.*

🍥 **FIELD NOTES** *These are very simple to prepare, but look fancy. The best way to crush the candy canes is to place them in a heavy-duty zipper-top plastic bag, then use a rolling pin to alternately roll over them and whack them. You can also try crushing them in a food processor fitted with a metal blade, but it will make a huge racket!*

🍥 **LIFESPAN** *Cupcakes may be baked 2 days ahead; frosted cupcakes are best served the same day. Store refrigerated in airtight container.*

Yield: *18 minty cupcakes*

 INGREDIENTS

18 white or Christmas-themed paper
  liners
1¾ cups crushed red-and-white
  peppermint candy canes (pieces should
  be no larger than ¼ inch)
1 batch batter from Chocolate Cupcakes
  (page 20)

1 batch Italian Meringue Buttercream
  (page 32)
7 ounces white chocolate, melted and
  slightly cooled
Pastry bag
Large star tip

 DIRECTIONS

1. Preheat oven to 350°F. Place paper
   liners in all wells of one 12-cup and
   one 6-cup cupcake tin.

2. Fold ¾ cup of the crushed candy canes
   into batter. Divide batter evenly among
   cupcake wells. Bake for about 22 minutes, or until a toothpick inserted in
   the center shows a few moist crumbs.
   Cool pans on racks for 5 minutes, then
   remove cupcakes to cooling racks to
   cool completely.

3. Place the buttercream in a large
   mixing bowl and beat in the

cooled melted white chocolate. Using
pastry bag fitted with tip, frost each
cupcake with a large swirl on top.
Sprinkle remaining 1 cup crushed
candy canes on top of cupcakes.
Cupcakes are now ready to serve.

Cupcake Tips

You can add more color by
using any of the various colored
candy canes available in stores. Some
are red, green, and white, which is fine. Just
be sure they are still peppermint, because
some are fruit flavored, and that just won't
do for this recipe! You may also simply
spread the frosting on top with an
icing spatula, rather than using
a pastry bag.

Christmas Tree Cupcakes

🎄 **HOLIDAY** *Christmas*

🧁 **DESCRIPTION** *The fun part of these cupcakes is the "Christmas tree" on top, which is an ice cream cone that kids can decorate. These are great to serve at a Christmas party. You can present the cones plain, so that the kids can frost them and affix the "decorations," or you can frost them yourself and let the little ones take it from there. Wilton Icing Color in Leaf Green lends the frosting that Christmas-tree color.*

🧁 **FIELD NOTES** *Very young children might need help applying the green frosting to the cone. Once that is done, the real fun starts! Sprinkle with glitter, arrange "ornaments," and place a star on top!*

🧁 **LIFESPAN** *Cupcakes may be baked 2 days ahead; frosted cupcakes are best served the same day. Store at room temperature in airtight container.*

Yield: *10 tree-topped cupcakes*

INGREDIENTS

10 panettone paper liners
1 batch batter from Yellow Cupcakes (page 19)
2 batches Classic Confectioners' Sugar Frosting (page 26; may be made all at once)
10 sugar cones (the type with the pointed ends)
Green food coloring

Pastry bag and coupler
Wilton tip #67 or other small leaf-shaped tip
Assorted colors of cake decorating gel
Green edible glitter, such as Wilton Cake Sparkles
Cinnamon red-hot candies for decoration
Small edible sugar confetti and star-shaped decorations

DIRECTIONS

1. Preheat oven to 350°F. Place panettone liners on a jelly-roll pan.

2. Divide batter evenly among liners. Bake for about 22 minutes, or until a toothpick inserted in center shows a few moist crumbs. Cool pan on rack for 5 minutes, then remove cupcakes to rack to cool completely. Trim tops, if necessary, to make level with liners.

3. Frost each cupcake with untinted white frosting using an icing spatula or a spoon. You can ice it smoothly, or make it look like snowdrifts.

4. Place ice cream cones on top of cupcakes, with pointed ends up.

5. Tint remaining frosting a good Christmas tree color with the green coloring. Fill pastry bag fitted with tip with frosting. Start at bottom of cones and pipe "branches" so that their pointed tips point downward. Go around and around the cone, moving upward to completely cover the cone, as in photograph.

6. Now go to town! Make garland swags with decorating gels. Sprinkle with glitter. Arrange red-hot "ornaments" any which way. Don't forget an edible tree topper! Cupcakes are now ready to serve.

Cupcake Tips

Baking the cupcakes in the panettone paper liners gives you a large base to support your "tree." The liners can be mail-ordered from Beryl's (see Resources).

105

Christmas Ornament Cupcakes

🧁 **HOLIDAY** *Christmas*

🧁 **DESCRIPTION** *Basic white or yellow cupcakes are topped with fondant glaze. Rolled fondant, cut out into Christmas tree ornament shapes and placed on top, is then personalized with colors and patterns of your choice.*

🧁 **FIELD NOTES** *Prepare these through step 3 and present them at a holiday party. Everyone—kids and adults—can decorate their own. Wilton Brush-On Color makes decorating these very easy and fun. The cookie cutter can be ordered from Sweet Celebrations (see Resources), or you can cut the fondant out freeform. The edible silver powder can be found in baking supply stores or ordered from Beryl's (see Resources).*

🧁 **LIFESPAN** *Cupcakes may be baked 2 days ahead; frosted cupcakes are best served the same day. Store at room temperature in airtight container.*

Yield: *23 ornamental cupcakes*

INGREDIENTS

23 white paper liners
1 batch batter from White Cupcakes
(page 18) or Yellow Cupcakes (page 19)
1 batch white Poured Fondant Glaze
(page 34)
Confectioners' sugar
8 ounces rolled white fondant, such as
Wilton Pure White Rolled Fondant

1¾-inch round ornament-shaped cookie
cutter
Wilton Brush-On Color in assorted
colors of your choice
Small, soft artist's brushes
Edible silver powder
Vodka

DIRECTIONS

1. Preheat oven to 350°F. Place paper liners in 23 wells of two 12-cup cupcake tins.

2. Divide cupcake batter evenly among paper liners. The liners will be only about one-third full (so there is headroom for the poured glaze later on). Bake for about 16 minutes, or until a toothpick inserted in the center shows a few moist crumbs. Cool pans on racks for 5 minutes, then remove cupcakes to racks to cool completely.

3. Use a teaspoon to aim the fluid fondant in the center of each cupcake, applying enough so that it spreads out on its own and flows to the edges of the liners. Make sure to cover cake completely while fondant is still fluid. Allow to dry, which will take just a few minutes. If you can still see the cake, or if the center of the cupcake is peaked, simply glaze a second time, adding enough fondant to create a smooth, flat, opaque surface. Allow to set and dry.

4. Sprinkle work surface with confectioners' sugar. Roll out a piece of rolled fondant to between ⅛ and ¼ inch thick. Using cookie cutter, cut out Christmas-ornament shapes. Use a large icing spatula to help loosen ornaments from work surface. Place an ornament on top of each cupcake.

5. Squirt individual colors of Brush-On Color into separate small dishes. Use brushes to paint patterns on fondant ornament. Thoroughly wash brushes in clean water and pat dry before using for another color. Allow ornaments to dry.

6. Place about a teaspoon of silver powder in a small bowl. Add vodka, a couple of drops at a time, stirring with brush until the silver forms a paint-like consistency. Paint the ornament "tops" as in photo. Cupcakes are now ready to serve.

Gilded Chocolate Flower Cupcakes

HOLIDAY *Bridal showers*

DESCRIPTION *A simple cupcake, brushed with an orange liqueur syrup, is crowned with Italian Meringue Buttercream and, the* pièce de résistance, *a handcrafted chocolate flower. You can choose to leave the flowers plain, or edge them with edible gold or silver powder.*

FIELD NOTES *The key to this recipe is the chocolate flowers. You might have to practice a few to get the hang of it, but the chocolate plastic can be reused, and the flowers can be made far ahead of time. The rose petal and leaf cutters can be purchased from Beryl's (see Resources). Also, when working with chocolate plastic I like to use a very small silicone rolling pin, which is available at cake-decorating supply stores, such as Beryl's, as is the edible gold and silver powder.*

LIFESPAN *Cupcakes may be baked 2 days ahead; frosted cupcakes are best served the same day. Store refrigerated in airtight container.*

108

Yield: *24 gilded cupcakes*

INGREDIENTS

1 batch Chocolate Plastic (page 111)
Confectioners' sugar
1½-inch rose petal–shaped cookie cutter
1-inch rose leaf–shaped cookie cutter
2-inch rose leaf–shaped cookie cutter

Orange syrup:
⅓ cup sugar
⅓ cup water
2 tablespoons Grand Marnier
2 tablespoons frozen orange juice
  concentrate, defrosted

24 cupcakes of your choice (I suggest
  white, yellow, or pound cake) in white or
  pastel paper liners
1½ batches Italian Meringue Buttercream
  (page 32; may be made all at once)
2 teaspoons Grand Marnier
1 teaspoon vanilla extract
Edible gold or silver powder
Vodka
Small, soft artist's brush

DIRECTIONS

1. To make the chocolate plastic roses, cut off about a golf ball–size piece of chocolate plastic and knead until soft. If it is very hard, hold it in your palms for a minute or two to warm it up. Roll out to ⅛-inch thickness on surface dusted with confectioners' sugar. Cut out 4 petals with the rose petal cutter to make small, tight roses. Cut out 7 to 10 petals for larger roses. (It is nice to make assorted sizes.) Use a small offset spatula to remove petals from work surface. Use fingers or rolling pin to smooth out the broad edge of each petal; the thinner the better.

2. To form the rose's center, take one petal and hold the center top of the petal between your index finger and thumb. With your other hand, gently but tightly roll the upper right-hand part of the petal diagonally toward the middle. The top will be the tip and should be tighter and narrower. When you get to the middle, remove your thumb and finger and continue

folding. You should have a cone shaped "center."

3. Take one of the petals and gently pinch the bottom, which will make the petal more of a curved, cup shape. The petal's top edge should be thinned out. Gently bend this top edge toward the back, forming a tight outward furl. Asymmetry is desirable and realistic. Repeat with remaining petals.

4. To begin attaching petals, place one petal against the cone base with the pinched end down. Flatten one side against the cone, leaving the other side open and away from the cone. Place one edge of the second petal in the middle of the first petal and flatten it against center. Your third petal will start in the center of the second petal and then be tucked under the first. These three petals, formed over the center, create a small rosebud. You may add additional petals, each beginning in the middle of the one

before. The more you add the larger the rose will become in diameter.

5. If the base of the rose is thick, trim any excess chocolate plastic from the base with a sharp paring knife. You want to coax the base into a reverse cone shape. This end will be nestled into buttercream and under chocolate plastic leaves, so it doesn't have to be perfect. You can also roll the bottom back and forth between your fingers to create this narrow shape. You may bend the petals inward or outward and mold them into any shape that you want. Brush off any excess confectioners' sugar with a soft brush. Place roses in airtight container in a single layer. They may be used immediately or stored for up to 1 month in a cool dry place.

6. To make the chocolate plastic leaves, roll out chocolate plastic as described above. Cut out smaller and larger leaf shapes. Use the edge of a sharp knife to imprint "veins." Store as above.

7. To make the orange syrup, stir sugar and water together in a small saucepan. Bring to a boil over medium-high heat. Swirl pot around to help dissolve sugar. Remove from heat and cool to room temperature. Stir in Grand Marnier and orange juice concen-

trate. Syrup is ready to use. (Syrup may be refrigerated in airtight container for up to 1 week.)

8. Place cupcakes on jelly-roll pans. Pierce each several times with a bamboo skewer. Brush orange syrup over each one, then go over each one again for maximum absorption.

9. Place the buttercream in a large mixing bowl and beat in Grand Marnier and vanilla extract. Frost each cupcake smoothly with the buttercream, using an icing spatula or a spoon. Place a rose on top of each cupcake, pressing the base gently down into the buttercream. Arrange a leaf or two around and beneath the rose. The leaves may be gently shaped for a more realistic look.

10. Place about a teaspoon of gold or silver powder in a small bowl. Add vodka, a couple of drops at a time, stirring with brush until it forms a paint-like consistency. Using brush, paint the edges of the rose and leaves with gold or silver, as desired. Cupcakes are now ready to serve.

Cupcake Tips

If, after you have let it sit until firm, the chocolate plastic is still either too hard or too soft to roll out and shape, make a note and adjust the amount of corn syrup next time. Also, if you are going to store your "plastic," place the well-wrapped piece in a zipper-top plastic bag, removing any air.

Chocolate Plastic

This funny-sounding decorating ingredient is simply a mixture of chocolate and corn syrup, and the result is malleable chocolate candy clay with a plastic-like resilience. It is perfect for making roses, leaves, and ribbons. Different brands of chocolate will yield different results. I have suggested that you use Wilton Candy Melts (see Resources), as they give reliable results. Also, since they are not "real" chocolate (having no cocoa butter in them), they make a chocolate plastic that is easier to work with. Cocoa butter melts at body temperature and, therefore, a chocolate plastic made with real chocolate will soften very quickly from the warmth of your hands. Occasionally, I have kept a bag of Wilton Candy Melts around for a while, and they do not seem to melt smoothly when not fresh. So for best results, buy them as you need them. Chocolate Plastic will keep for 2 weeks at room temperature in an airtight container.

Yield: *about 2 pounds*

INGREDIENTS

28 ounces Wilton Candy Melts in White, finely chopped

⅔ cup light corn syrup

DIRECTIONS

1. Melt the Wilton Candy Melts in the top of a double boiler or in the microwave. Stir in the corn syrup until the mixture comes together. It might look grainy, but that is typical at this stage. Scrape out onto a large piece of plastic wrap and wrap up well.

2. Let sit for at least 6 hours at cool room temperature, or until firm enough to roll out, preferably overnight. Chocolate plastic is ready to use.

Basket-of-Flowers Cupcakes

🌸 **HOLIDAY** *Bridal showers*

....

🌸 **DESCRIPTION** *These cupcakes feature yellow cake, lemon curd filling, and Italian Meringue Buttercream piped in a basketweave pattern on the outside. Fresh flowers of your choice adorn the top.*

....

🌸 **FIELD NOTES** *Consider serving these at an intimate lunch or dinner party hosted for a shower. Place them on your prettiest plates! Make sure to use edible flowers, such as miniature roses or pansies, and obtain them from a source that can assure you that they are free of pesticides. Try asking at a farmers' market or using flowers from a private garden. If you are worried, place a round of parchment on top of the mini cakes and place the flowers on top of that; simply remove them before eating the cupcakes. You need the panettone paper liners to get the right shape for these cupcakes. If you have a cake-decorating turntable, the basketweave piping will be much easier.*

....

🌸 **LIFESPAN** *Cupcakes may be baked 2 days ahead; frosted cupcakes are best served the same day. Store refrigerated in airtight container.*

Yield: *10 flower-topped basketweave cupcakes*

INGREDIENTS

10 panettone paper liners
1 batch batter from Yellow Cupcakes (page 19)
1 batch lemon curd (see page 57)
Pastry bag and coupler
Ateco or Wilton tip #12, or any plain round tip with approximately ¼-inch opening

2 batches Italian Meringue Buttercream (page 32)
1 tablespoon vanilla extract
Ateco tip #47
Ateco or Wilton tip #18 or other small star tip
10 gorgeous open roses (or more, if desired)

DIRECTIONS

1. Preheat oven to 350°F. Place panettone liners on a jelly-roll pan.

2. Divide batter among liners. Bake for about 22 minutes, or until a toothpick inserted in center shows a few moist crumbs. Cool pan on rack for 5 minutes, then place cupcakes directly on rack to cool completely.

3. Trim tops of cupcakes, if necessary, to make level with papers. Carefully peel liners away and discard.

4. Place lemon curd in pastry bag fitted with #12 tip. Insert tip right down into the center of each cupcake. Squeeze to fill with lemon curd. As soon as the top or sides of the cupcake begins to expand, ease up on pressure. If any lemon curd is oozing out of the top, simply wipe away before frosting. Place each cupcake on a pretty serving plate.

5. Place the buttercream in a large mixing bowl and beat in vanilla extract. Use an icing spatula to smoothly cover tops of cupcakes with buttercream first. Then, place buttercream in pastry bag fitted with #47 tip. Using the ridged side of the tip, pipe a vertical line going from the bottom of the cupcake to the top. Then pipe about 3 horizontal lines, each approximately 1 inch long, across the vertical line, equally spaced from top to bottom. The number will depend on the exact height of the cupcake. Make the first horizontal line along the top edge of the cake. The next line will be one line's width down from it, and so on, until you reach the bottom of the cupcake. (Refer to the photo for guidance.) Pipe a second vertical line to the right of the horizontal lines, overlapping those edges. Then pipe more horizontal lines across this vertical line, filling in the spaces formed by the previous horizontal lines. Repeat this pattern, working all around the cupcake. As you approach the end, space it so that the last set of horizontal lines complements the first set. They should dovetail and fit together neatly.

6. Switch to tip #18 and pipe a shell or reverse shell border on top outer edge of cupcake. Chill cupcakes until buttercream firms up. Bring back to room temperature before serving. Place flower(s) on top of cupcake. Cupcakes are now ready to serve.

Bride and Groom Cupcakes

🧁 **HOLIDAY** *Weddings*

🧁 **DESCRIPTION** *Yellow or white cupcakes are topped with white and chocolate fondant glaze. Further embellishment is provided by rolled fondant cut out into shapes to make "clothes," which are decorated with piped icing. There are 23 cupcakes to decorate, so someone has to be the odd man (or woman) out. If you are associated with one side or the other, then you can tilt the scales!*

🧁 **FIELD NOTES** *These are all about the decoration. Just roll out your fondant and use a sharp knife to cut out shapes using your best judgment. Feel free to experiment with different necklines for the ladies: scoop neck, ballet neck, V-neck, heart-shaped neck, etc. Once placed on the cupcakes, you can adjust the shapes by nudging the fondant into place or trimming further. The pearl dust is a dry type of coloring that can be found through cake-decorating supply stores such as Beryl's (see Resources). Applied to rolled fondant with a dry brush, it gives a pretty sheen.*

🧁 **LIFESPAN** *Cupcakes may be baked 2 days ahead; frosted cupcakes are best served the same day. Store at room temperature in airtight container.*

Yield: *23 formally attired cupcakes*

 INGREDIENTS

23 paper liners (it's nice to have white for the "brides" and black or brown for the "grooms")

1 batch batter from White Cupcakes (page 18) or Yellow Cupcakes (page 19)

1 batch Poured Fondant Glaze (page 34; half white and half chocolate)

8 ounces rolled fondant, such as Wilton Pure White Rolled Fondant

Confectioners' sugar

Small, soft artist's brush

Pearl dust

Wilton Icing Writer in White

2 ounces semisweet chocolate, melted

Parchment cone

 DIRECTIONS

1. Preheat oven to 350°F. Place paper liners in 23 wells of two 12-cup cupcake tins.

2. Divide batter evenly among 23 paper liners. The liners will be only one-third full (so there is headroom for the poured glaze later on). Bake for about 16 minutes, or until a toothpick inserted in the center shows a few moist crumbs. Cool pans on racks for 5 minutes, then place cupcakes directly on racks to cool completely.

3. Glaze the cupcakes in the white liners with the white poured fondant and the cupcakes in the dark liners with the chocolate poured fondant. Use a teaspoon to aim the fluid fondant into the center of each cupcake, applying enough so that it spreads out on its own and flows to the edges of the liners. Make sure to cover cake completely while fondant is still fluid. Allow to set and dry, which will take just a few minutes. If you can still see the cake, or if the center of the cupcake is peaked, simply glaze a second time, adding enough fondant to create a smooth, flat, opaque surface. Allow to dry.

4. You will be cutting out long triangles of rolled fondant for the men's tuxedoes and necklines of dresses for the brides. You might want to sketch out desired shapes with pencil and paper first. Sprinkle work surface with confectioners' sugar. Roll out a piece of fondant to between ⅛ and ¼ inch thick. Use a small, thin-bladed sharp knife to cut out shapes as needed. Use a small offset spatula to remove pieces from work surface. Place on cupcakes as desired. You will now have the "shirt" on the groom's cakes and the "dress" bodice on the bride's. Push rolled fondant into place or trim as necessary. Use a dry brush to apply pearl dust to the wedding dress.

5. Use Icing Writer to make a pearl necklace on the ladies and outline the neckline, if desired. Allow to dry. Place melted chocolate in parchment cone. Snip a very small opening. Pipe bow tie and buttons on the men. Chill briefly to set chocolate. Cupcakes are now ready to serve.

Sugared Flowers Cupcakes

 **HOLIDAY** *Weddings*

 **DESCRIPTION** *Here, cupcakes in the flavor of your choice are covered with a vanilla buttercream, and then each cupcake wears a perfectly gorgeous, edible, crystallized flower.*

 **FIELD NOTES** *These can be served individually, but a display stand makes them wedding cake–like and perfect for a small wedding reception, rehearsal dinner, or shower. The stand I use is the Wilton Cupcakes 'N More Dessert Stand, which holds 23 cupcakes. You can always have more cupcakes behind the scenes for serving a larger crowd. Just double or triple the recipe as needed. Make sure to buy edible flowers and leaves that are not sprayed or treated. A friend's garden or a farmers' market is a good bet. The superfine sugar can be found in the supermarket baking aisle.*

 **LIFESPAN** *Cupcakes may be baked 2 days ahead; frosted cupcakes are best served the same day. Store refrigerated in airtight container.*

Yield: *23 flower-topped cupcakes*

 INGREDIENTS

Crystallized flowers:

30 small (1- to 2-inch diameter) edible
flowers such as pansies, Johnny-jump-ups,
small roses, or rose petals
45 edible leaves, such as scented geranium
2 cups superfine sugar
2 large egg whites
Tweezers
Small, soft artist's brush

23 cupcakes of your choice (yellow, white,
or pound cake is perfect) in white or
pastel paper liners
1½ batches Italian Meringue Buttercream
(page 32; may be made all at once)
1½ tablespoons vanilla extract
Pastry bag
Large star tip

 DIRECTIONS

1. To make the crystallized flowers and
leaves, make sure flowers and leaves
are dry. You want perfect specimens
without any blemishes, nicks, or cuts.
Place sugar in a small bowl. Whisk egg
whites until frothy in another small
bowl.

2. Hold the base of the flower or leaf
with tweezers or your fingertips. Use
the brush to coat every surface, top
and bottom, with egg white. You want
a thin, even coat. Make a thorough
coat, because you cannot successfully
go back and redo after the sugar is
applied.

3. Hold the flower or leaf over the bowl
of sugar. Use a teaspoon to scoop up
the sugar and sprinkle it evenly over
the flower or leaf. The sugar will
adhere to the egg white. Shake gently to see if any areas still need
sugar, and sprinkle sugar where
needed. Place flower or leaf on cooling rack to dry. Repeat with other
flowers and leaves. They should dry at
least overnight, or until completely dry
and crisp. If you have a gas oven with

a pilot light, place rack in oven to
speed drying.

4. Place cupcakes on a work surface.
Place buttercream in large bowl and
beat in vanilla extract. Fill the pastry
bag with the frosting and, using the tip,
make a small swirl on top of each cupcake as shown in photograph. Gently
press a flower and a leaf or two onto
frosting. Cupcakes are now ready to
serve. (You may refrigerate them for
most of the day, but make sure to bring
back to room temperature before serving.) To arrange in stand, simply posi-
tion one cupcake in
each well of the
stand.

Cupcake Tips

You can also purchase
exquisite candied flowers
and leaves from
Meadowsweets (see
Resources), a company
devoted to this art.

Fruit "Tart" Cupcakes

🟣 **HOLIDAY** *Baby showers*

🟣 **DESCRIPTION** *These take their inspiration from the beautiful, fancy fruit tarts with pastry cream filling in the bakery. Here, white cupcakes are filled with pastry cream, then topped with fruit and a shiny glaze.*

🟣 **FIELD NOTES** *Berries (sliced strawberries or whole blueberries, raspberries, or blackberries) work particularly well for these "tarts." I have also made these with a few slices of kiwi on top or thinly sliced peaches, nectarines, or apricots arranged in a fan shape. The apple jelly is relatively clear and mild in flavor and works with any fruit. It you like, you could use strained apricot jam for the stone fruits or red currant jelly for the red fruits. One attractive way to individualize these is to use varied color paper liners and then match them to the fruit: green liners for kiwi, blue for blueberries, pink for raspberries, and so on.*

🟣 **LIFESPAN** *Cupcakes may be baked 2 days ahead; glazed cupcakes are best served the same day. Store refrigerated in airtight container.*

Yield: *24 tart-like cupcakes*

 INGREDIENTS

Pastry cream:
1⅓ cups milk
1 vanilla bean
4 large egg yolks
⅓ cup sugar
Pinch of salt
Generous 3 tablespoons all-purpose flour

2 batches White Cupcakes (page 18)
  in paper liners of your choice
Pastry bag and coupler
Ateco or Wilton Tip #12 (or any plain
  round tip with approximately ¼-inch
  opening)
1½ cups apple jelly
Enough fruit of your choice to top 24
  cupcakes (see Cupcake Tips)

DIRECTIONS

1. To make the pastry cream, place milk in a medium-size nonreactive pot. Split vanilla bean down center and scrape all of the tiny seeds into the milk. Add the vanilla bean to the milk as well. Bring to a boil over medium heat. Remove from heat, but keep warm. Let bean steep for 15 minutes.

2. Meanwhile, whisk the egg yolks and sugar together in a large bowl until creamy. Whisk in salt and flour until smooth.

3. Remove the vanilla bean from the milk. Reheat milk until it just comes to a simmer. Pour about one-quarter of the warm milk over the egg yolk mixture, whisking gently. Add remaining milk and whisk to combine. Immediately pour mixture back into the pot and whisk continuously over low-medium heat until thickened, about 8 minutes, but do not let it boil. The pastry cream should be thick enough to mound when dropped from a spoon.

4. Allow pastry cream to cool; stir frequently to release heat. When almost at room temperature, scrape into airtight container and refrigerate for at least 4 hours or until thoroughly chilled.

Pastry cream may be made up to 3 days ahead.

5. If the cupcake tops are very peaked, trim to make a level surface. Place pastry cream in pastry bag fitted with tip. Insert tip right down into the center of each cupcake. Squeeze to fill with cream. As soon as the top of the cupcake begins to expand and crack, ease up on pressure—the cupcake has taken on as much filling as it can. If any pastry cream is oozing out of the top, simply wipe away before topping.

6. Heat jelly in small saucepan over low heat or in microwave until very fluid. Brush jelly over cupcakes to make a sticky surface. Arrange fruit, either whole or sliced, on top of cupcake. Fill the surface as much as possible with fruit. Brush jelly over fruit and cupcake surface. Chill to set jelly. Cupcakes are now ready to serve.

Cupcake Tips

Here's the approximate amount of fruit needed per cupcake: 1 strawberry; 12 raspberries; 10 blackberries; 15 blueberries; ½ of a kiwi or apricot; ¼ of a peach or nectarine.

Chocolate Turtle Cupcakes

HOLIDAY *Baby showers*

DESCRIPTION *The basic brownie cupcake recipe is enhanced with caramel, pecans, and bittersweet chocolate ganache to make a cupcake with the flavors of chocolate turtle candies.*

FIELD NOTES *Anything with chocolate and caramel is worth eating, as far as I am concerned. And if the mom-to-be craves chocolate, these will definitely satisfy her! While the basic recipe for brownie cupcakes yields 18, by the time you add all the extra nuts, chips, and caramel in this recipe, you end up with 2 dozen cupcakes.*

LIFESPAN *Cupcakes may be baked 2 days ahead; glazed cupcakes are best served the same day. Store at room temperature in airtight container.*

Yield: *24 candy-like cupcakes*

 INGREDIENTS

24 brown paper liners
24 Kraft caramels
1 cup semisweet chocolate morsels
1 batch batter from Brownie Cupcakes
(page 25)

1 batch Ganache Glaze and Frosting
(page 28)
⅔ cup pecan halves, toasted (see page 13)
and chopped

DIRECTIONS

1. Preheat oven to 350°F. Place paper liners in all wells of two 12-cup cupcake tins.

2. Chop 12 of the caramels into ¼-inch dice. If the caramel is sticky, spritz your knife with nonstick cooking spray. Fold chopped caramels and chocolate morsels into the cupcake batter. Divide batter evenly among cupcake wells. Bake for about 25 minutes, or until a toothpick inserted in center shows many moist crumbs. Cool pans on racks for 5 minutes, then remove cupcakes to cooling racks to cool completely.

3. Melt remaining 12 caramels in top of double boiler or in microwave. Rewarm ganache if necessary to bring it to a fluid state. Drizzle melted caramel over tops of cupcakes using a fork or teaspoon. Sprinkle with some of the nuts while caramel is still sticky. Drizzle ganache with fork or teaspoon over all and top with remaining nuts. Chill cupcakes briefly, until caramel and ganache are set. Cupcakes are now ready to serve.

Cupcake Tips

The caramel, nut, and ganache toppings can be layered repeatedly until you have as decadent a topping as you desire. Depending on how decadent you are, you might want extra caramels, nuts, and ganache.

Key Lime Coconut Cupcakes

🧁 **HOLIDAY** *Graduations*

🧁 **DESCRIPTION** *These begin with yellow cupcakes enhanced with a tart lime curd filling. They are topped with vanilla frosting and then covered with toasted coconut, which gives them flavor and crunch. If you can find key limes, use them, but regular limes work great too.*

🧁 **FIELD NOTES** *These tropical flavors make me think of warm days, hence their designation as a cupcake for graduations, which are traditionally in May or June. Of course, they would also certainly be welcomed in the midst of winter to bring a tropical flavor to a cold day. Make the lime curd a day ahead to give it a chance to chill. And although the coconut takes just a few minutes to toast, it also can be prepared ahead and stored at room temperature for 1 week.*

🧁 **LIFESPAN** *Cupcakes may be baked 2 days ahead; frosted cupcakes are best served the same day. Store at room temperature in airtight container.*

Yield: *24 tropical-flavor cupcakes*

INGREDIENTS

Lime curd:
¼ cup freshly squeezed key lime juice
2 large eggs
1 large egg yolk
¾ cup sugar
6 tablespoons (¾ stick) unsalted butter, at room temperature, cut into pieces

3 cups sweetened flaked coconut
Pastry bag and coupler
Ateco or Wilton Tip #12 (or any plain round tip with approximately ¼-inch opening)
2 batches Yellow Cupcakes (page 19) in white paper liners
1 batch Classic Confectioners' Sugar Frosting (page 26)

DIRECTIONS

1. To make the lime curd, place key lime juice, eggs, egg yolk, and sugar in a small heavy-bottomed saucepan. Whisk together until thoroughly combined. Place over low-medium heat and whisk occasionally until mixture begins to thicken. Do not let it simmer or boil, or the eggs will curdle. Whisk in butter a piece at a time. Continue to cook until mixture is thick enough to mound when dropped by a spoon, about 10 minutes. Remove from heat, let cool to room temperature, and refrigerate in airtight container at least overnight or up to 1 week.

2. Preheat oven to 350°F. Sprinkle coconut onto jelly-roll pan in single layer and bake until most of it is light golden brown, about 5 minutes. Shake the pan at least once during baking time. Cool on a rack.

3. Place lime curd in pastry bag fitted with tip. Insert tip right down into the center of each cupcake. Squeeze to fill with lime curd. As soon as the top of the cupcake begins to expand and crack, ease up on pressure—the cupcake has taken on as much filling as it can. (Aim for about 1 tablespoon filling per cupcake.) If any lime curd is oozing out of the top, simply wipe away before frosting.

4. Frost cupcakes using an offset spatula or teaspoon. Use about 2 tablespoons of frosting per cupcake and there will be just enough. After frosting, hold each cupcake over the jelly-roll pan and use cupped palm and fingers to cover frosting completely with coconut. Excess coconut will fall back onto pan and can be reused. Cupcakes are now ready to serve.

Strawberry Cheesecake Cupcakes

HOLIDAY *Graduations*

DESCRIPTION *Vanilla cheesecake is sandwiched between a layer of yellow cake on the bottom and luscious strawberries with a shiny glaze on top. These are great for parties because you can make the cupcakes the day before and chill them overnight before topping them with the berries.*

FIELD NOTES *I didn't know if the yellow cake batter and the cheesecake batter would bake properly at the same time. But, luckily for all of us, they did, and the results are easy, creamy, and delicious. You could top these with other berries, such as blueberries or raspberries, if you like. These cupcakes keep well and can be made well ahead.*

LIFESPAN *Cupcakes may be baked 3 days ahead or frozen for up to 1 week; glazed cupcakes are best served the same day. Store refrigerated in airtight container.*

124

Yield: *24 berrylicious cupcakes*

 INGREDIENTS

24 paper liners of your choice

Cheesecake:
16 ounces cream cheese, at room
  temperature
1 cup confectioners' sugar
1 teaspoon vanilla extract

1 batch batter from Yellow Cupcakes
  (page 19)
24 whole strawberries
1⅓ cups apple jelly

DIRECTIONS

1. Preheat oven to 350°F. Place paper
   liners in all wells of two 12-cup
   cupcake tins.

2. To make the cheesecake, in a large
   bowl with an electric mixer on
   medium-high speed, beat cream cheese
   until creamy, about 2 minutes. Add
   confectioners' sugar and vanilla extract
   and beat until smooth and creamy,
   about 3 minutes, scraping down the
   bowl once or twice; set aside.

3. Divide the cupcake batter among the
   24 cupcake wells. Top with cheesecake
   batter, dividing equally over the cake
   batter. Bake for about 20 minutes. The
   cheesecake might crack a little, which
   is okay. The tops should look puffed
   and dry. They will not color.
   Cool cupcake tins on racks.
   Refrigerate at least overnight, still in cupcake tins.

4. Remove cupcakes from tins and place
   on jelly-roll pan to catch drips from the
   subsequent topping. Rinse and pat
   strawberries dry. Hull them, then slice
   from top to bottom in very thin
   slices—the thinnest they can be without
   falling apart. Fan out slices on top of
   cupcakes in whatever attractive patterns you like—like a flower, straight
   across, fan shaped, etc.

5. Heat jelly in small saucepan over
   low heat or in microwave until very
   fluid. Brush jelly over strawberries
   and cupcake surface. Chill to set jelly.
   Cupcakes are now ready to serve.

Cupcake Tips

I love the new easy-to-
clean silicone pastry brushes.
They are perfect for brushing
on the jelly coating—no more
bristles left behind sticking
to your baked goods!

Chocolate Hazelnut Cupcakes

🧁 **HOLIDAY** *Adults' birthdays*

🧁 **DESCRIPTION** *These cupcakes will truly satisfy the chocolate-hazelnut lovers out there. The chocolate cupcake batter is enhanced with ground hazelnuts, and the cupcakes are dressed up with Nutella filling, chocolate buttercream, and gianduja curls. They are sophisticated and decadent.*

🧁 **FIELD NOTES** *You could certainly make these round, but I like them in a square shape, for which you will need a special pan, available through King Arthur Flour The Baker's Catalogue (see Resources). If you use a traditional round tin, you will get 18 cupcakes rather than 12. The regular round paper liners will fit into the square tins. Nutella, a chocolate hazelnut spread, can be found next to the peanut butter in the supermarket. The gianduja is a specialty chocolate—a blend of chocolate and hazelnuts—that is softer than most chocolates, so it is easy to shave curls off of a block with a vegetable peeler.*

🧁 **LIFESPAN** *Cupcakes may be baked 2 days ahead; frosted cupcakes are best served the same day. Store refrigerated in airtight container.*

Yield: *12 hazelnut-rich cupcakes*

INGREDIENTS

12 brown paper liners
½ cup hazelnuts, toasted and skinned (see page 13)
1 batch batter from Chocolate Cupcakes (page 20), prepared with ½ cup less flour
1 cup Nutella, at room temperature
Pastry bag and coupler

Ateco or Wilton tip #12 (or any plain round tip with approximately ¼-inch opening)
½ batch Italian Meringue Buttercream (page 32)
4 ounces bittersweet chocolate, melted and slightly cooled
One 6-ounce block gianduja

DIRECTIONS

1. Preheat oven to 350°F. Place paper liners in all wells of one 12-cup square cupcake tin.

2. Place nuts in work bowl of a food processor fitted with a metal blade. Pulse on and off to chop, then process until finely ground. Blend hazelnuts into cupcake batter. Divide batter evenly among cupcake wells. The batter will come up about three-quarters of the way to top of liners. Bake for about 25 minutes, or until a toothpick inserted in center shows a few moist crumbs. Cool pan on rack for 5 minutes, then remove cupcakes to a cooling rack to cool completely.

3. Place Nutella in pastry bag fitted with #12 tip and insert tip right down into the center of each cupcake. Squeeze to fill with Nutella. As soon as the top of the cupcake begins to expand and crack, ease up on pressure—the cupcake has taken on as much filling as it can. (Aim for about 1 generous tablespoon filling per cupcake.) If any Nutella is oozing out of the top, simply wipe away before frosting.

4. Place the buttercream in a large mixing bowl, and beat in the cooled melted bittersweet chocolate. Frost cupcakes using an icing spatula or a spoon.

5. Make gianduja curls by using a vegetable peeler to shave curls off of the block of gianduja. Sprinkle curls on top of cupcakes. Cupcakes are now ready to serve.

Chocolate Raspberry Blackout Cupcakes

🍰 **HOLIDAY** *Adults' birthdays*

🍰 **DESCRIPTION** *Bite into rich chocolate cake frosted with luxurious fresh raspberry–dark chocolate buttercream. Chocolate cake crumbs envelop the outside.*

🍰 **FIELD NOTES** *I grew up in New York City, where blackout cake was very common bakery fare. It was a combination of chocolate cake and chocolate frosting (sometimes pudding-like), and it was always covered with chocolate cake crumbs all over the outside. With the addition of the raspberry flavor, these are my little blackout tributes! I like to make these in square cupcake tins, available through King Arthur Flour The Baker's Catalogue (see Resources) so they look more sophisticated for a grown-up birthday. The yield is approximate, as you might end up making crumbs out of one or two of the extra cupcakes—believe me, it is worth it!*

🍰 **LIFESPAN** *Cupcakes may be baked 2 days ahead; frosted cupcakes are best served the same day. Store refrigerated in airtight container.*

128

Yield: *8 blackout cupcakes*

 INGREDIENTS

1 batch batter from Chocolate Cupcakes (page 20)

1 batch Italian Meringue Buttercream (page 32)

½ cup fresh or defrosted and well-drained frozen raspberries

7 ounces bittersweet chocolate, melted and slightly cooled

 DIRECTIONS

1. Preheat oven to 350°F. Coat the insides of one 12-cup square cupcake tin with nonstick cooking spray.

2. Divide cupcake batter evenly among the wells. Bake for about 25 minutes, or until a toothpick inserted in center shows a few moist crumbs. Cool pan on rack for 5 minutes, then remove cupcakes to a cooling rack to cool completely.

3. Trim off the peaked tops (soon to be the bottoms) of the cupcakes. Place trimmings in a bowl and crumble finely with your hands. You should have about 1 cup. Take 4 of the cupcakes and crumble them into the bowl as well.

4. Place the buttercream in a large mixing bowl. Beat in the raspberries and the cooled melted bittersweet chocolate.

5. Turn all of the cupcakes upside down so the broad end is now the bottom. Generously frost tops and all sides of the cupcakes using an icing spatula or a spoon. Gently press cake crumbs all over cupcakes (see photo). Chill briefly to set buttercream; return to room temperature before serving. Cupcakes are now ready to serve.

Cupcake Tips

To further embellish these, crown each one with a single, perfect fresh raspberry.

Chocolate Drizzle Cupcakes

🧁 **HOLIDAY** *Adults' birthdays*

🧁 **DESCRIPTION** *Straight-sided chocolate cupcakes are topped with whipped cream frosting and chocolate ganache drizzled on the top and down the sides. With fresh raspberries and mint leaves crowning these elegant birthday treats, who needs candles?*

🧁 **FIELD NOTES** *I saw a picture of a huge cake with a frosting and glaze just like this in a fabulous book called* The Pastry Queen *by Rebecca Rather (Ten Speed Press, 2004). I figured, why not create a cupcake version? These are best served on a plate with a spoon. I like to make these with straight-sided cupcake tins; the ones I use are the flexible silicone style and make unmolding very easy. You can mail-order them from Complements to the Chef (www.complementstothechef.com). Make sure the raspberries are very firm and dry.*

🧁 **LIFESPAN** *Cupcakes may be baked 2 days ahead; glazed cupcakes are best served the same day. Store refrigerated in airtight container.*

Yield: *18 sophisticated chocolate-packed cupcakes*

 INGREDIENTS

1 batch Chocolate Cupcakes (page 20), made without paper liners
2 batches Whipped Cream Frosting (page 30; may be made all at once)

1 batch Ganache Glaze and Frosting (page 28)
18 fresh whole raspberries
18 fresh small mint leaves

DIRECTIONS

1. Trim any peaks off the tops of the cupcakes to make them level. Although the cupcakes should be straight sided and flat on both ends, I like to use the bottoms as the tops, because they will be perfectly flat and easier to frost.

2. Place the cupcakes bottom side up and, using a small offset icing spatula, spread the frosting generously all over the tops and sides. The cupcakes are very light and might move around; use a very light hand and the frosting process will be easier. Chill for 1 hour, or until frosting has set and firmed up a bit.

3. Have ganache in a fluid state, but not too warm. Use a tablespoon to aim ganache straight down on top center of cupcake. Use the back of the spoon, if necessary, to encourage the glaze to partially drip down the sides (see photo). Place a raspberry and a mint leaf on top. Chill until serving time, up to 6 hours. Cupcakes are now ready to serve.

Wacky Faces Cupcakes

🧁 **HOLIDAY** *Kids' birthdays*

🧁 **DESCRIPTION** *Blond or brunette, girl or boy, subtle smile or toothy grin, faces of all descriptions will emerge on these cupcakes. Once the fondant "face" is put into place, kids and party guests can make their own facial features and hair with various frostings and decorations.*

🧁 **FIELD NOTES** *Prepare these through step 4 and present them at your child's party. Have one cupcake for each child, and have available an assortment of frostings and decorations. Make one for them so they can see some of the possibilities. I have left the facial "skin" white to keep them a blank canvas, so to speak. For skin color ideas, see Cupcake Tips (opposite).*

🧁 **LIFESPAN** *Cupcakes may be baked 2 days ahead; frosted cupcakes are best served the same day. Store at room temperature in airtight container.*

Yield: *23 expressive cupcakes*

 INGREDIENTS

23 white paper liners
1 batch batter from White Cupcakes (page 18) or Yellow Cupcakes (page 19)
1 batch Poured Fondant Glaze (page 34)
Confectioners' sugar
8 ounces white rolled fondant, such as Wilton Pure White Rolled Fondant
2¼-inch round cookie cutter

Assorted colors of Wilton Icing Writer, Icing Tubes, and Gel Tubes
Assorted star and round tips (to attach to above icings)
Coupler rings, same number as chosen icings
Assorted sprinkles, edible confetti, glitter, etc., for decoration

 DIRECTIONS

1. Preheat oven to 350°F. Place paper liners in 23 wells of two 12-cup cupcake tins.

2. Divide batter evenly among liners. The liners will be only one-third full (so there is headroom for the poured glaze). Bake for about 16 minutes, or until a toothpick inserted in center shows a few moist crumbs. Cool pans on racks for 5 minutes, then remove cupcakes to cooling racks to cool completely.

3. Use a teaspoon to aim the fluid fondant into the center of each cupcake, applying enough so that it spreads out on its own and flows to the edges of the liners. Make sure to cover cake completely while fondant is still fluid. Allow to set and dry, which will take just a few minutes. If you can still see the cake, or if the center of the cupcake is peaked, simply glaze a second time, adding enough fondant to create a smooth, flat, opaque surface. Allow to set and dry.

4. Sprinkle work surface with confectioners' sugar. Roll out a piece of rolled fondant to between ⅛ and ¼ inch thick. Cut out 23 2¼-inch circles. Use a large icing spatula to help loosen circles from work surface. Place a circle of

fondant on top of each cupcake. Cupcakes are now ready for decoration.

5. Begin with hair. Using black, brown, or yellow tube icing fitted with star tip, make a hairstyle around the top of the "face." Or use a round tip to pipe individual hairs. The Icing Writer is great for hair and any features that demand small details. Use round tips to make eyes, nose, and mouth features, or use a dot of icing to affix decorations, such as small round confetti for eyes. Use a little red or pink gel to make "blush"! Encourage creativity! Make an alien girl or boy with green blush, red eyes, and purple hair, if you like! Cupcakes are now ready to serve.

Cupcake Tips

If you would like to make the "faces" realistic skin colors, have some Wilton Copper, Brown, and Ivory Icing Colors on hand. By using any of these straight or mixing them, you can approximate most skin colors. Simply knead them, bit by bit, into the rolled fondant before rolling it out.

Colorful Confetti Cupcakes

🧁 **HOLIDAY** *Kids' birthdays*

🧁 **DESCRIPTION** *You choose whatever cupcake batter that you (or your child) like for these cupcakes. The key is the colorful edible spray and the Wilton Cupcakes 'N More Dessert Stand (see Resources) to present the cupcakes in a festive way.*

🧁 **FIELD NOTES** *There are many readily available decorator tools that can make cupcake decorating that much easier—so why not take advantage? Some examples are the new edible spray colors and this amazing display stand. The odd number of cupcakes refers to the fact that the stand holds 23 cupcakes. You can use any type of candles; I like the kind that glow in the dark!*

🧁 **LIFESPAN** *Cupcakes may be baked 2 days ahead; frosted cupcakes are best served the same day. Store at room temperature in airtight container and arrange in stand at last minute.*

Yield: *23 very colorful cupcakes*

INGREDIENTS

1½ batches Classic Confectioners' Sugar
Frosting (page 26; may be made all at
once)
Pastry bag
Large star tip
23 cupcakes of your choice in paper liners
of your choice

Wilton Color Mist edible spray color in an
assortment of colors
Small edible sugar confetti decorations
Wilton Cupcakes 'N More Dessert Stand
23 small birthday candles

DIRECTIONS

1. Place the frosting in the pastry bag fitted with the tip, and make a large,
   multilayered swirl of frosting on top of
   each cupcake.

2. Spray cupcakes with edible spray. You
   can either keep each one an individual
   color or make them multicolored.
   Sprinkle with confetti.

3. Arrange cupcakes on stand; insert candles. Cupcakes are now ready to serve.

In the Pink Cupcakes

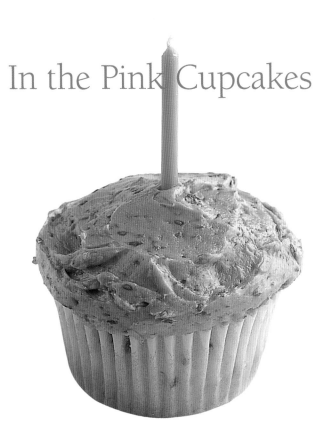

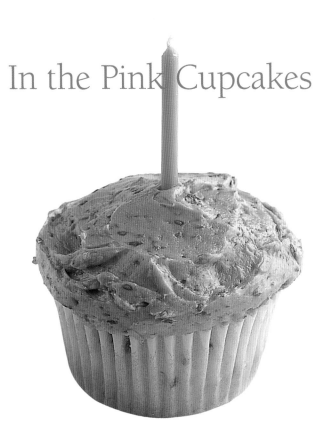 **HOLIDAY** *Kids' birthdays*

....

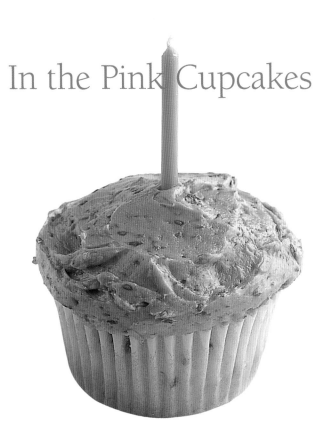 **DESCRIPTION** *White cupcake batter gets fresh raspberries folded into it. The Italian Meringue Buttercream also gets a dose of fresh raspberries to make a very pink—and delicious—frosting.*

....

 FIELD NOTES *You can make these cupcakes with fresh or frozen raspberries. If you are using frozen, make sure to defrost and drain them well. You want only the berries, not the drained liquid. These are great for a girl's summer birthday—just add pink candles.*

....

 LIFESPAN *Cupcakes may be baked 2 days ahead; frosted cupcakes are best served the same day. Store refrigerated in airtight container.*

Yield: *14 pretty pink cupcakes*

 **INGREDIENTS**

14 pink paper liners
1½ cups fresh or defrosted and well-drained frozen raspberries
1 batch batter from White Cupcakes (page 18)

½ batch Italian Meringue Buttercream (page 32)
14 pink candles

DIRECTIONS

1. Preheat oven to 350°F. Place paper liners in 14 wells of one 12-cup and one 6-cup cupcake tin.

2. Fold ¾ cup raspberries into cupcake batter. Divide batter evenly among paper liners. Bake for about 20 minutes or until edges are turning light golden brown; a toothpick inserted in the center will show a few moist crumbs. Cool pans on racks for 5 min-utes, then remove cupcakes to cooling racks to cool completely.

3. Beat remaining ¾ cup raspberries into the buttercream. The buttercream will turn pink and you will see bits of fruit suspended here and there. Frost cupcakes smoothly using an icing spatula or a spoon. Insert a candle into each cupcake. Cupcakes are now ready to serve.

Caramel Popcorn Brownie Cupcakes

🧁 **HOLIDAY** *Kids' birthdays*

🧁 **DESCRIPTION** *The basic brownie cupcake recipe is topped with caramel popcorn, more caramel, and chocolate ganache for a gooey treat.*

🧁 **FIELD NOTES** *There are many caramel-style popcorns on the market, but I use Cracker Jack. The preparation technique for these cupcakes is very different: When you pull the hot brownie cupcakes out of the oven, you immediately press the caramel popcorn down into the warm, soft cake.*

🧁 **LIFESPAN** *Cupcakes may be baked 2 days ahead; topped cupcakes are best served the same day. Store at room temperature in airtight container.*

Yield: *18 gooey, chewy cupcakes*

INGREDIENTS

18 paper liners of your choice
1 batch batter from Brownie Cupcakes,
  prepared without the pecans (page 25)
3⅓ cups caramel popcorn, such as
  Cracker Jack

18 Kraft caramels
1 batch Ganache Glaze and Frosting
(page 28)

DIRECTIONS

1. Preheat oven to 350°F. Place paper liners in all wells of one 12-cup and one 6-cup cupcake tin.

2. Divide cupcake batter evenly among wells. Bake for about 25 minutes, or until a toothpick inserted in center shows many moist crumbs. The tops will be dry and crackled in appearance and slightly puffed.

3. As soon as the cupcakes come out of the oven, while they are still in their tins, press an even, single layer of caramel popcorn down into the brownies to cover the top surface. About half of each kernel should now be embedded in the brownie (this will be about 2

tablespoons of popcorn per cupcake). Cool pans on racks for 5 minutes, then remove cupcakes to cooling racks to cool completely.

4. Melt caramels in top of double boiler or in microwave. Have ganache in a fluid state. Using a fork or teaspoon, drizzle caramel over tops of popcorn. Drizzle about 2 teaspoons of ganache with fork or teaspoon over each cupcake. Chill cupcakes briefly until caramel and ganache are set. Cupcakes are now ready to serve.

Cupcake Tips

You will have some ganache left over, but it freezes very well, for up to 1 month in an airtight container.

Dirt and Worms Cupcakes

🟤 **HOLIDAY** *Kids' birthdays*

🟤 **DESCRIPTION** *Chocolate cake plus chocolate frosting and ground chocolate cookies for dirt make for a "dirty" looking cupcake. Add gummy worms creeping out of the "dirt" and you have a perfect cupcake for children's birthdays.*

🟤 **FIELD NOTES** *The title might sound yucky, but these are really quite tasty—particularly for the younger kids.*

🟤 **LIFESPAN** *Cupcakes may be baked 2 days ahead; frosted cupcakes are best served the same day. Store at room temperature in airtight container.*

Yield: *18 "dirty" cupcakes*

 INGREDIENTS

1 batch Chocolate Cupcakes (page 20) in brown paper liners
1½ batches Fudge Frosting (page 27; may be made all at once)

1¾ cups ground chocolate cookie crumbs (I use Nabisco Famous Chocolate Wafers)
36 gummy worms

DIRECTIONS

1. Frost each cupcake generously using an icing spatula or a spoon. Place chocolate cookie crumbs in a wide bowl. Hold each cupcake over the bowl. Using a spoon or your fingers, scoop up crumbs and sprinkle over the frosting to cover completely. You want the surface to look like dirt. (Excess crumbs will fall back into the bowl and can be reused.)

2. Place gummy worms artfully on cupcakes so that they are emerging from the "dirt." Use about 2 worms per cupcake. I like cutting the worms in half and burying the cut halves down into the cupcake so that the worms are emerging from the dirt (see photo). Cupcakes are now ready to serve.

Hostess with the Mostest Cupcakes

🧁 **HOLIDAY** *Kids' bake sales*

....

🧁 **DESCRIPTION** *Just like the commercially prepared version with the similar name, these cupcakes start with chocolate cake and have a creamy vanilla filling. A chocolate glaze goes on top, which is then decorated with white frosting squiggles. If you want to be true to the original, make sure there are seven squiggly loops on each cupcake.*

....

🧁 **FIELD NOTES** *This cupcake is a perfect example of how the master recipes in this book can be combined to produce a singular creation. I hope you will mix and match to your heart's content to come up with your own tasty ideas.... You might just come up with the next iconic flavor combination and signature look! Note that you will have some Classic Confectioners' Sugar Frosting left over.*

....

🧁 **LIFESPAN** *Cupcakes may be baked 2 days ahead; glazed cupcakes are best served the same day. Store at room temperature in airtight container.*

Yield: *18 chocolatey, squiggly cupcakes*

INGREDIENTS

1 batch Classic Confectioners' Sugar
   Frosting (page 26)
Pastry bag and coupler
Ateco or Wilton Tip #12 (or any plain
   round tip with approximately ¼-inch
   opening)

1 batch Chocolate Cupcakes (page 20)
   in brown paper liners
1 batch Ganache Glaze and Frosting
   (page 28)
Ateco or Wilton Tip #3

DIRECTIONS

1. Place confectioners' sugar frosting in
   pastry bag fitted with #12 tip and
   insert tip right down into the center of
   each cupcake. Squeeze to fill with frosting. As soon as the top of the cupcake
   begins to expand and crack, ease up on
   pressure—the cupcake has taken on as
   much filling as it can. (Aim for about 1
   tablespoon filling per cupcake.) If any
   frosting is oozing out of the top, simply
   wipe away before glazing. Cupcakes
   may be made up to this point early in
   the day of serving.

2. Rewarm ganache if necessary to bring
   it to a fluid state. Use a small offset
   spatula or a teaspoon to apply about 1
   tablespoon of ganache to the top of
   each cupcake; cover the top smoothly
   with ganache. Place confectioners'
   sugar frosting in pastry bag fitted with
   #3 tip, and pipe seven loopy squiggles
   across the top of each cupcake, as
   shown in photograph. Chill cupcakes
   briefly until glaze is set. Cupcakes are
   now ready to serve.

Chocolate Chip Marbled Fudge Cupcakes

HOLIDAY *Kids' bake sales*

DESCRIPTION *This recipe uses the recipe for Marbled Cupcakes, which are a variation on the Yellow Cupcakes. I have added miniature semisweet chocolate morsels to the cake batter for an added dose of chocolate. If that weren't enough, the cupcakes are crowned with Fudge Frosting and a candy decoration that looks like a very mod, '60s-ish flower.*

FIELD NOTES *Kids of all ages love these, so they should sell quite well at a bake sale. They would also be welcomed at birthday parties. Because of their fun nature, I like to bake these in colorful, patterned paper liners (I especially like the Wilton Flower Power style), but of course this can be varied at whim.*

LIFESPAN *Cupcakes may be baked 2 days ahead; frosted cupcakes are best served the same day. Store at room temperature in airtight container.*

Yield: *12 very kid-friendly cupcakes*

 INGREDIENTS

12 colorful paper liners
½ cup miniature semisweet chocolate morsels
1 batch batter from Marbled Cupcakes (see Variation, page 19)

1 batch Fudge Frosting (page 27)
12 Wilton Flower Power Icing Decorations (optional)

DIRECTIONS

1. Preheat oven to 350°F. Place paper liners in all wells of one 12-cup cupcake tin.

2. Fold chocolate morsels into the half of the cupcake batter that is still yellow. Divide the two batters evenly among the cupcake wells and marble (swirl) as directed.

3. Bake for about 18 minutes, or until a toothpick inserted in the center shows a few moist crumbs. The center should also spring back when lightly pressed. Cool pan on rack for 5 minutes, then remove cupcakes to a cooling rack to cool completely.

4. Frost each cupcake smoothly and generously using an icing spatula or a spoon (use photo as guidance). Crown each cupcake with sugar decorations, if desired. Cupcakes are now ready to serve.

Peanutty Chocolate Cupcakes

🥜 **HOLIDAY** *Kids' bake sales*

🥜 **DESCRIPTION** *There had to be a cupcake in this book combining the great flavors of peanuts and chocolate. Here a chocolate cupcake gets a peanut butter filling, a fudge frosting, and a sprinkling of dry-roasted peanuts.*

🥜 **FIELD NOTES** *You will get different results when using different peanut butters. If you use a natural peanut butter (no sugar added, no hydrogenated fat), you will get a more peanutty-tasting filling, but it will be less smooth. If you use a commercial peanut butter, the filling will be silky smooth, but sweeter. So it's your choice.*

🥜 **LIFESPAN** *Cupcakes may be baked 2 days ahead; frosted cupcakes are best served the same day. Store at room temperature in airtight container.*

Yield: *18 nutty, chocolatey cupcakes*

🧁 INGREDIENTS

18 brown paper liners
½ cup peanut butter
6 tablespoons confectioners' sugar
Pinch of salt
1 batch batter from Chocolate Cupcakes
(page 20)

Pastry bag
Large star tip
1½ batches Fudge Frosting (page 27;
may be made all at once)
¾ cup salted dry-roasted peanuts,
chopped

🧁 DIRECTIONS

1. Preheat oven to 350°F. Place paper liners in all wells of one 12-cup and one 6-cup cupcake tin.

2. In a large bowl with an electric mixer on medium-high speed, beat peanut butter until creamy, about 2 minutes. Add confectioners' sugar and salt and beat until smooth and combined, about 3 minutes, scraping down the bowl once or twice.

3. Fill each cupcake well about one-quarter of the way full with chocolate cupcake batter. Place about 1 teaspoon of peanut butter mixture in the center, then fill the wells with the remaining batter.

4. Bake for about 22 minutes, or until a toothpick inserted into the cake portion of the cupcake shows a few moist crumbs. Cool pans on racks for 5 minutes, then remove cupcakes to cooling racks to cool completely.

5. Using pastry bag fitted with tip, pipe a swirl of frosting on top of each cupcake. Sprinkle each cupcake with some peanuts. Cupcakes are now ready to serve.

Cupcake Tips

These are even easier to make if you forgo the pastry bag and tip and simply apply frosting with an icing spatula or teaspoon.

Black and White Cupcakes

 **HOLIDAY** *Kids' bake sales*

 **DESCRIPTION** *These graphic-looking cupcakes use both white and chocolate fondant glaze to top off white or yellow cupcakes.*

 **FIELD NOTES** *These look like the black and white cookies that are popular in many New York–area bakeries. Their attraction is their offering of two of the greatest flavors, so you don't have to pick just one or the other.*
You will be preparing the fondant glaze as described in the Cupcake Tips section of that recipe, making half of it into a chocolate flavor.

 **LIFESPAN** *Cupcakes may be baked 2 days ahead; frosted cupcakes are best served the same day. Store at room temperature in airtight container.*

Yield: *23 dual-flavor cupcakes*

 INGREDIENTS

23 white paper liners
1 batch batter from White Cupcakes (page 18) or Yellow Cupcakes (page 19)

1 batch Poured Fondant Glaze, half chocolate and half white (page 34)

 DIRECTIONS

1. Preheat oven to 350°F. Place paper liners in 23 wells of two 12-cup cupcake tins.

2. Divide batter evenly among paper liners. The liners will be only one-third full (so there is headroom for the poured glaze later on). Bake for about 16 minutes, or until a toothpick inserted in center shows a few moist crumbs. Cool pans on racks for 5 minutes, then remove cupcakes to cooling racks to cool completely.

3. Make sure chocolate fondant is just pourable and not too liquid. Use a teaspoon to drizzle chocolate fondant in a vertical line across the center of each cupcake, dividing it in half. Fill half of it with the chocolate fondant. Allow to set and dry briefly. Fill other half with white fondant. Allow to set and dry. Cupcakes are now ready to serve.

Cookies 'n' Cream Cupcakes

 **HOLIDAY** *Kids' bake sales*

 **DESCRIPTION** *These are very easy to make: Yellow cupcakes and confectioners' sugar frosting, with crushed chocolate crème sandwich cookies mixed into both the batter and the frosting.*

 **FIELD NOTES** *To get the best flavor for these, use Oreo chocolate sandwich cookies. It seems that almost all kids, no matter their likes and dislikes, love Oreos. If you or your kids like cookies-and-cream ice cream, you are going to love these cupcakes.*

 **LIFESPAN** *Cupcakes may be baked 2 days ahead; frosted cupcakes are best served the same day. Store at room temperature in airtight container.*

Yield: *14 cookie-filled cupcakes*

 INGREDIENTS

14 paper liners of your choice

15 chocolate crème sandwich cookies (such as Oreos), chopped

1 batch batter from Yellow Cupcakes (page 19)

½ batch Classic Confectioners' Sugar Frosting (page 26)

 DIRECTIONS

1. Preheat oven to 350°F. Place paper liners in 14 wells of one 12-cup and one 6-cup cupcake tin.

2. Fold 1 cup chopped cookies into cupcake batter. Divide batter evenly among 14 paper liners. Bake for about 18 minutes, or until a toothpick inserted in the center shows a few moist crumbs. Cool pans on racks for 5 minutes, then remove cupcakes to cooling racks to cool completely.

3. Fold remaining chopped cookies into frosting. Frost cupcakes using an icing spatula or a spoon. Cupcakes are now ready to serve.

Malted Milk Ball Cupcakes

🧁 **HOLIDAY** *Kids' bake sales*

🧁 **DESCRIPTION** *Here yellow cupcakes are flavored with malt powder and enhanced with the added crunch of crushed malted milk balls. You'll find more malted milk balls in the frosting.*

🧁 **FIELD NOTES** *I use Ovaltine malt powder and Whoppers malted milk balls for this recipe. These cupcakes were inspired by the malted milk ball chocolate chip cookies in one of my companion books,* A Baker's Field Guide to Chocolate Chip Cookies *(The Harvard Common Press, 2004).*

🧁 **LIFESPAN** *Cupcakes may be baked 2 days ahead; frosted cupcakes are best served the same day. Store at room temperature in airtight container.*

Yield: *14 malted cupcakes*

 INGREDIENTS

14 paper liners of your choice
2 tablespoons Ovaltine malt powder
1 cup malted milk balls, such as Whoppers, finely chopped

1 batch batter from Yellow Cupcakes (page 19)
½ batch Classic Confectioners' Sugar Frosting (page 26)
14 whole malted milk balls

 DIRECTIONS

1. Preheat oven to 350°F. Place paper liners in 14 wells of one 12-cup and one 6-cup cupcake tin.

2. Thoroughly stir malt powder and ½ cup chopped malted milk balls into the cupcake batter. Divide batter evenly among paper liners. Bake for about 18 minutes, or until a toothpick inserted in the center shows a few moist crumbs. Cool pans on racks for 5 minutes, then remove cupcakes to cooling racks to cool completely.

3. Beat remaining chopped malted milk balls into frosting. Frost cupcakes using an icing spatula or a spoon. Top each cupcake with a single whole malted milk ball. Cupcakes are now ready to serve.

Tutti-Frutti Nutty Buddy
Cupcakes

🧁 **HOLIDAY** *Kids' bake sales*

🧁 **DESCRIPTION** *Starting with basic carrot cake cupcakes, these have the addition of crushed pineapple, dried cherries or cranberries, poppy seeds, coconut, apricots, and pecans.*

🧁 **FIELD NOTES** *Trying to get kids to eat more healthy veggies, fruits, and nuts? They will love these cupcakes, which are also great for a breakfast treat! This recipe makes a lot of cupcakes, but they freeze pretty well due to the oil content, which keeps them moist. The unsweetened coconut can be found in the bulk section of natural foods markets.*

🧁 **LIFESPAN** *Cupcakes may be baked 1 week ahead and frozen, or baked 2 days ahead; frosted cupcakes are best served the same day. Store refrigerated in airtight container.*

Yield: *36 fruit and nut–filled cupcakes*

🌸 INGREDIENTS

36 paper liners of your choice

1½ cups pecan halves, toasted (see page 13) and chopped

1 cup chopped dried apricots

1 cup dried cranberries, chopped

½ cup crushed canned pineapple, drained

½ cup sweetened flaked or unsweetened dried coconut

¼ cup poppy seeds

1 batch batter from Carrot Cake Cupcakes, prepared without the walnuts (page 24)

2 batches Cream Cheese Frosting (page 29; may be made all at once)

🌸 DIRECTIONS

1. Preheat oven to 350°F. Place paper liners in all wells of three 12-cup cupcake tins.

2. Fold 1 cup of the pecans, ½ cup of the apricots, ½ cup of the cranberries, and the pineapple, coconut, and poppy seeds into the cupcake batter. Divide batter evenly among paper liners. Bake for about 16 minutes, or until a toothpick inserted in center shows a few moist crumbs. Cool pans on racks for 5 minutes, then remove cupcakes to cooling racks to cool completely.

3. Frost each cupcake generously with the frosting using an icing spatula or a spoon. In a small bowl, toss together remaining pecans, apricots, and cranberries. Sprinkle some on top of each cupcake. Cupcakes are now ready to serve.

S'mores Cupcakes

🔴 **HOLIDAY** *Kids' bake sales*

🔴 **DESCRIPTION** *What do you get when you combine chocolate cake, chocolate-covered graham crackers, and marshmallows? S'mores cupcakes, of course.
They are finished off with a swirl of browned meringue frosting, which mimics toasted marshmallow.*

🔴 **FIELD NOTES** *S'mores are most often made over the campfire during summer vacation, but kids will be delighted to have these sweet flavors at other times of year. With these you don't need a fire, but you do need a broiler or a crème brûlée torch to brown the marshmallow-like frosting.*

🔴 **LIFESPAN** *Cupcakes may be baked 2 days ahead; frosted cupcakes are best served the same day. Store at room temperature in airtight container.*

Yield: *22 campfire-ready cupcakes*

INGREDIENTS

22 brown paper liners
1⅓ cups coarsely chopped chocolate-
  covered graham crackers
1⅓ cups miniature marshmallows
1 batch batter from Chocolate Cupcakes
(page 20)

1 batch Fluffy Meringue Frosting (page 31)
Pastry bag
Large star tip

DIRECTIONS

1. Preheat oven to 350°F. Place paper liners in 22 wells of two 12-cup cupcake tins. Fold chopped graham crackers and marshmallows into cupcake batter. Divide batter evenly among 22 paper liners.

2. Bake for about 22 minutes, or until a toothpick inserted in the center shows a few moist crumbs. Cool pans on racks for 5 minutes, then remove cupcakes to racks to cool completely.

3. Place frosting in pastry bag fitted with the tip and make a large swirl on top of each cupcake as in photograph. Cupcakes may be made up to this point early in the day of serving.

4. Right before serving, run cupcakes under a hot broiler until meringue just becomes tinged with color. Alternatively, you may use a crème brûlée torch and simply wave it back and forth over the cupcakes. Cupcakes are now ready to serve.

Resources

Beryl's Cake Decorating and Pastry Supplies

P.O. Box 1584
North Springfield, VA 22151
(703) 256-6951
(800) 488-2749
FAX (703) 750-3779
www.beryls.com
There is a Beryl, who will often answer the phone herself, and provides highly personal and professional customer service. Look here for chocolates, rolled fondant, pastry bags, decorating tips, panettone paper liners (ask for cupcake size), deeply fluted brown paper liners (which are actually brioche molds), red and green foil liners, dark brown paper liners, gold and silver powders, gold leaf, pink "pearls," tiny 3-millimeter white pearl dragées, and more.

Chocosphere

(877) 99CHOCO
FAX (877) 992-4626
www.chocosphere.com
If you are looking for high-quality chocolate, make this your resource. This company specializes in all my favorite chocolates that are great to eat and to use in your baked goods. Owners Joanne and Jerry Kryszek offer excellent personal service, and they ship nationwide.

King Arthur Flour The Baker's Catalogue

58 Billings Farm Road
White River Junction, VT 05001
(800) 827-6836
FAX (802) 649-5359
www.kingarthurflour.com
This catalog, which is updated often, offers high-quality extracts, chocolates, scales, and excellent measuring cups, including ones in odd sizes. They also have the exclusive on a great square-shaped cupcake/muffin tin that I love. Also look here for a cupcake carrier called Cup-a-Cake. It carries one single frosted cupcake to school or work, keeping it fresh and uncrushed.

KitchenAid

P.O. Box 218
St. Joseph, MI 49085
(800) 541-6390
www.kitchenaid.com
Go directly to this Web site for a complete listing of their high-quality products. All of my cupcakes were baked with a KitchenAid stove and prepared with a KitchenAid mixer and food processor. I bought my mixer almost 20 years ago and it is still going strong—this is a worthwhile investment for any avid baker.

Meadowsweets

173 Kramer Road
Middleburgh, NY 12122
(888) 827-6477
www.candiedflowers.com
For exquisite crystallized flowers and leaves, call Toni Elling at Meadowsweets. Turn to this pro for the most beautiful candied roses, pansies, scented geranium leaves, and more.

New York Cake Supplies
56 West 22nd Street
New York, NY 10010
(212) 675-2253
(800) 942-2539
FAX (212) 675-7099
www.nycake.com
You can shop here for food coloring, colored sugars, nonpareils, cupcake tins, prepared rolled fondant, panettone liners, high-quality chocolates, and more.

Sur La Table
Catalog Division
P.O. Box 34707
Seattle, WA 98124
(206) 448-2244
(800) 243-0852
www.surlatable.com
Here you will find high-quality cupcake tins, heat-resistant spatulas, great measuring cups, and more. If you can visit one of their stores, you will find dozens of gorgeous platters and pedestal dishes on which to serve your cupcakes; call for locations.

Sweet Celebrations
P.O. Box 39426
Edina, MN 55439-0426
(800) 328-6722
www.sweetc.com
www.maidofscandinavia.com
This company offers a huge array of equipment and ingredients, such as cupcake tins, liners, pastry bags and decorating tips, great chocolates, confetti, sparkly decorations of all sorts, books, and more.

Williams-Sonoma
P.O. Box 7456
San Francisco, CA 94120
(800) 541-2233
FAX (415) 421-5253
www.williams-sonoma.com
Famous for their mail-order catalog, they also have stores nationwide. You will find well-made, accurate measuring tools; KitchenAid mixers; vanilla extract; some chocolate and cocoa products; and other baking equipment, including cupcake tins and icing spatulas of all sorts.

Wilton Industries, Inc.
2240 West 75th Street
Woodridge, IL 60517
(800) 794-5866
www.wilton.com
This company publishes a great catalog that offers equipment and ingredients, as well as visual inspiration for the baker. I love their nonstick cupcake tins. They are heavy duty and have great handles for gripping—perfect for maneuvering in and out of the oven. They also have paper liners in all types of colors and patterns, from solid colors to ones for most major holidays; prepared fondant; pastry bags and tips; food colors, colored sprays, and edible markers; and lots of sparkly decorations. Try their Cupcakes 'N More Dessert Stand for displaying your gorgeous creations, and also their Ultimate 3-in-1 Cake Caddy for transporting your cupcakes effortlessly (there are little round ridges to hold the cupcakes in place).

Measurement Equivalents

Please note that all conversions are approximate.

Liquid Conversions

U.S.	Metric
1 tsp	5 ml
1 tbs	15 ml
2 tbs	30 ml
3 tbs	45 ml
¼ cup	60 ml
⅓ cup	75 ml
⅓ cup + 1 tbs	90 ml
⅓ cup + 2 tbs	100 ml
½ cup	120 ml
⅔ cup	150 ml
¾ cup	180 ml
¾ cup + 2 tbs	200 ml
1 cup	240 ml
1 cup + 2 tbs	275 ml
1¼ cups	300 ml
1⅓ cups	325 ml
1½ cups	350 ml
1⅔ cups	375 ml
1¾ cups	400 ml
1¾ cups + 2 tbs	450 ml
2 cups (1 pint)	475 ml
2½ cups	600 ml
3 cups	720 ml
4 cups (1 quart)	945 ml (1,000 ml is 1 liter)

Weight Conversions

U.S./U.K.	Metric
½ oz	14 g
1 oz	28 g
1½ oz	43 g
2 oz	57 g
2½ oz	71 g
3 oz	85 g
3½ oz	100 g
4 oz	113 g
5 oz	142 g
6 oz	170 g
7 oz	200 g
8 oz	227 g
9 oz	255 g
10 oz	284 g
11 oz	312 g
12 oz	340 g
13 oz	368 g
14 oz	400 g
15 oz	425 g
1 lb	454 g

Oven Temperature Conversions

°F	Gas Mark	°C
250	½	120
275	1	140
300	2	150
325	3	165
350	4	180
375	5	190
400	6	200
425	7	220
450	8	230
475	9	240
500	10	260
550	Broil	290

Index